RJ505.P6 M683 1997
Moustakas, Clark E
Relationship play therapy

D1266973

Relationship
Play Therapy

D.N.C. AT ASHEVILLE
ASHEVILLE, NC 28804

Relationship
Play Therapy

Clark Moustakas

JASON ARONSON INC.
Northvale, New Jersey
London

D. HIDEN RAMSEY LIBRARY
U.N.C. AT ASHEVILLE
ASHEVILLE, NC 28804

Production Editor: Elaine Lindenblatt

This book was set in 11 pt. Bulmer by Alpha Graphics of Pittsfield, New Hampshire, and printed and bound by Book-mart Press of North Bergen, New Jersey.

Copyright © 1997 by Wendy Moustakas

10 9 8 7 6 5 4 3 2 1

All rights reserved. No part of this book may be used or reproduced in any manner whatsoever without written permission from Jason Aronson Inc. except in the case of brief quotations in reviews for inclusion in a magazine, newspaper, or broadcast.

Library of Congress Cataloging-in-Publication Data
Moustakas, Clark E.
    Relationship play therapy / Clark Moustakas.
       p. cm.
    Includes bibliographical references and index.
    ISBN 0-7657-0029-8 (alk. paper)
    1. Play therapy. 2. Therapeutic alliance. I. Title.
    [DNLM: 1. Play Therapy. 2. Psychotherapy—case studies. WS
350.2 M933r 1997]
RJ505.P6M683 1997
618.92'891653—dc20
DNLM/DLC
for Library of Congress   96-9434

Printed in the United States of America on acid-free paper. For information and catalog write to Jason Aronson Inc., 230 Livingston Street, Northvale, New Jersey 07647-1731. Or visit our website: http://www.aronson.com

For Wendy Moustakas

*Through the years
continuing light and love*

Contents

Preface

Relationship Play Therapy presents the experiences of children in therapy—children generally happy and secure, and children coping with disturbing problems in relationships within their family and with other significant people in their everyday world. The book delineates applications of play therapy principles, values, and methods that are used in specialized play situations to help children express tensions and frustrations and become freer and more alive. It presents examples of children suddenly or temporarily disturbed in their family life and tells how these children work out their fear and anger in a few play therapy sessions. It describes more seriously disturbed children in play therapy: their struggles to achieve emotional maturity, and their growing faith in themselves, acceptance of their life situations, and respect for other people.

This book contains transcriptions of child–therapist communications in play therapy. These verbatim stories and the discussions that follow provide readers with an opportunity to understand children and their problems, and to respond more effectively.

The material in this volume has been shared with students, parents, and teachers. Many have stated that it awakened new perspectives of children's behavior and experiences and inspired them to reexamine their own relations with children.

Perhaps as much as at any time in human history, children are being neglected, controlled, and abused in violent homes, neighborhoods, and in society. Abuse and violence exist everywhere, deterring, distorting, and harmfully redirecting children's natural purposes, resources, and interests, undermining self-expression and self-affirmation.

A recent special publication of the Mott Foundation (1996) concerning youth and violence reported that in 1992, homicide was the second leading cause of death for 15- to 24-year-olds and that in 1990 the number of lives lost to firearm injuries totaled 20.4 billion. Among the striking conclusions of the report: violence begins in early childhood and can be predicted as likely in adulthood by the age of 8. The report also observed that youths avoid crime not out of fear of punishment but out of respect for themselves, respect for others, and optimism about the future. Among the solutions offered in the report: a violence prevention/conflict resolution curriculum, a program for building self-esteem, and a plan for dealing with feelings of loss and anxiety connected with victimization.

My hope is that *Relationship Play Therapy* will reawaken the true meaning of respect, acceptance, and love for children, the valuing of their uniqueness, and the support of their common destinies. A major purpose of the book is to point to play therapy possibilities and meanings of play that will move children toward gentleness and cooperation and away from forces that promote hostility, violence, and crime.

Acknowledgments

I especially want to recognize Garry Landreth, Center for Play Therapy, University of North Texas, whose questions and comments inspired me to revisit the roots and unfoldings of my work as a play therapist. Dr. Landreth's recent videotaping of my play therapy sessions with individual children and with a small group awakened new visions and meanings of my life with children and inspired the creation of *Relationship Play Therapy*.

I express my appreciation to Drs. Colleen McNally and Alvin Ramsey, psychology professors, and Jill Benton, Librarian, Center for Humanistic Studies, for their inspiring comments and support of my work with children and families; and to Wendy Moustakas, my daughter, and Betty Moustakas, my wife, who contributed loving affirmations along the way and influenced my decision to revisit play therapy. I also thank Vange Puszcz, Center for Humanistic Studies, for her magical energy and assistance in preparing this book for publication.

Clark Moustakas
January 1997

1

Relationship Play Therapy

*F*rom the earliest years of my life, play has fascinated me. My pre-school years were filled with hours of playful fantasies, imaginative wonderings and wanderings. Living in a small, crowded home with my parents and four siblings, I learned at an early age how to expand my home space. Through internal visions and fanciful connections to earth, wind, and stars, I discovered a universal space of infinite and timeless meaning.

Early Play Connections

I learned at a very early age to be at home in darkness, to enter freely and comfortably into unknown forces and callings, to welcome new, serendipitous mysteries of nature and people, and a wide range of sounds and sights. I often took an untrodden path, and pursued risky ventures in spite of warnings and cautions that I was in danger and bound to suffer severe consequences.

I deliberately traveled the back roads to school, daring to change my course every week in order to explore and enjoy varied forms of life—

1

trees, shrubs, weeds, and flowers. I faced numerous barriers and learned to cope with adversity. As I moved along the way, I sought to find strange rocks, and relics of various kinds. I was entranced by everything, noticing what existed before me, what mattered to me, what provided material for my learning, thinking, imagining, and writing.

In elementary and high school, I completed assignments quickly, often without interest or involvement. I wanted free time, purposeful time, to pursue internal pathways of consciousness, to enter into playful daydreams and creations of imagination, ritual and myth, tales of far-off places. In these vision quests, there were always barriers to overcome and challenges to master, as well as the wonder and beauty of an open, free, receptive, interior life.

Play Therapy Beginnings

My professional interest in play began with studies at the Merrill-Palmer Institute in Detroit in 1946 and 1947. I found myself completely absorbed in children's worlds and their play, learning much more about children directly from them than from my graduate courses and books on child psychology and child development.

From the very first day I entered the Merrill-Palmer preschool, children surrounded me and drew me into their play. Immediate, magical connections awakened between us, not only with individual children but with the entire group. We moved in a single orbit, creating play dramas and constructions with ordinary materials—wood, nails, paper, crayons, paints, sand, water, family puppets. The materials offered limitless possibilities for the individual child and for shared moments. They inspired stories and profound, wondrous encounters. I became a versatile participant in children's plays. Through play, I soon understood, appreciated, and valued each child. I witnessed directly the child's powers and resources for problem solving and for shaping and directing life rather than being determined by it. Play was the source and the strategy for coming to terms with the challenges of being, relating, and living as a unique and incomparable child or as a distinctive member of a group.

I learned early in my life with children that I could count upon my own perceptiveness, compassion, and receptiveness to guide children's growth and development. I discovered that I had resources of inventiveness and ways of stretching my own boundaries to help children find themselves. I saw what excited, entranced, and captivated a child. I understood the profound significance of recognizing children's interests and desires for an imaginative life. I learned how to facilitate children's freedom through verbal and silent expression. I was particularly drawn to children who were alone, angry, frightened, lonely, and who faced life with disabilities. The unique child stood out for me. I became a source of energy for nourishing, enriching, and responding to a child's invitations and offerings.

Within the first few months of my play experiences in the preschool setting of Merrill-Palmer, though rich in resources and possibilities, I realized that the setting did not provide opportunities for sustained, uninterrupted play with individual children or with small groups of children. To advance my knowledge and competencies, I enrolled in a graduate course in play therapy taught by Dr. Amy Holway. Through my observations and studies, and Dr. Holway's guidance, I began my work as a play therapist. Soon, I found that her cognitive-behavioral theories and methods were not congruent with my spontaneity and interactional ways of being with children, or my belief in children's powers to direct and shape their own destinies in play and problem solving. Dr. Holway not only accepted my ideas but encouraged me to be myself as a child therapist, and utilize my own way of being with children. With her support during a six-month timespan, I met with individual children and small groups of children in a play therapy room. I took my cues from the children, entering into their world on invitation—not imposing a theory or methodology aimed at shaping their behavior or directing their play.

My interest in and proclivity toward play as a medium for self-engagement are rooted in my personal history and especially my early childhood years, my on-the-way-to-school journeys and at-home dramas. Looking back, I see myself sitting on the front steps of my home. I remember watching elements of life in my neighborhood, especially play activities, when and where they occurred, their nature, content, and unfolding. I often was joined by neighborhood children. We created stories, sketches, and games that awakened exuberant energy and instructed us on ways of being and relating, ways to inventiveness and imaginative dramas.

When I began my professional work as a play therapist, my guiding mentors were Carl Rogers and Virginia Axline. I had studied their writings while I was a graduate student at Wayne State University and the Merrill-Palmer Institute.

Later, as a doctoral student at Teachers College, Columbia University, I formally became a student of Virginia Axline, enrolled in her play therapy course, studied her articles on play therapy, and worked with individual children under her supervision. Then, in my first year as a faculty member at Merrill-Palmer, Virginia came to Detroit, met with my students, and presented a series of talks on play therapy research and practice. She inspired and encouraged me to continue my work as a nondirective play therapist.

When I accepted a full-time faculty position at Merrill-Palmer, I was to be a colleague of Dr. Amy Holway, my first play therapy guide. About a month before I was to join her, she became seriously ill and suddenly died. I was faced with the sole responsibility of the Merrill-Palmer play therapy program. Amy was not only my first teacher but a friend whom I had come to trust unconditionally and to love. I missed her deeply and felt the loss of her guidance and friendship.

In my meetings with children during those first years of independent work as the professional play therapist at Merrill-Palmer, I applied the nondirective approach in content, thoughts, and feelings, concentrating on children's verbal communications. Their play constructions were the focus of my attention. Wanting to become a competent play therapist, I tape recorded every interview and studied the verbatim transcripts in order to understand and advance my effectiveness.

Becoming a Relationship Play Therapist

As the months unfolded, I became increasingly restless and uncomfortable with nondirective ways of responding to children in play therapy. I saw during two years of intensive practice that sitting in a chair, observing, and reflecting the content of children's play, or their thoughts and feelings, were not consistent with my way of being with people. I had been an active participant in my life with children and in my own play creations. How had I come to think that to be successful as a professional play therapist I had to suppress my natural bent for interactive communication, to fix my eyes, my body, my full attention on the other person? I realized that I had been carrying out a role, defined by others, not by me or the children with whom I met. I had not fully used my knowledge, talents, and experiences or my resources and strategies for entering into the world of childhood. Gradually, in the early years of teaching play therapy, I learned from children, their parents, and my students' questions how to be more effective. I came to insights that extended and deepened my competencies and skills, my ability not only to understand the immediate wishes, meanings, and constituents of a child's play but also to see where a child was heading in the resolution of an issue or challenge. As I studied the tape-recorded sessions and reflected on my experiences with children in play and play therapy, I became convinced that the essential ingredients of change were rooted in the interactions between child and therapist, in the developing relationship.

During this period, from my research data and reflections, and from the verbatim examples, a relationship therapy model of play therapy began to take shape. The essential conditions, structures, and boundaries of play and play therapy became clearer to me. With an unusual spontaneity and commitment, I became fully absorbed in describing the essential conditions and the therapeutic process of play therapy. I saw that the attitudes of the therapist were as important as the therapist's accurate understanding of a child's behavior and play experience. I completed a manuscript (1953) on child therapy, emphasizing the values of faith, acceptance, and respect in play with children and in play therapy.

In the early fifties, only a small group of psychologists was practicing play therapy. The work of psychologists largely involved psychological testing and some psychotherapy with adults. Today, play therapy is an international enterprise. Literally thousands of psychologists, social workers, psychiatrists, and counselors include play therapy in their services. An international association of play therapists exists, international conferences are held yearly, and an international journal is published by the Association of Play Therapy.

As I developed as an independent practitioner, I continued systematically to study and analyze verbatim tape recordings of my interviews with children. I developed and published research papers on play therapy. I saw in every interview the importance of conversation, dialogue, mutuality, person-to-person interaction. Thus, my therapy with children became fully established as *relationship therapy*.

I had left behind nondirective play therapy as a model but continued to reflect feelings and content of children's verbal and silent expressions when such responses were appropriate. However, when I met with a child, I was always conscious of the fact that, from the very first moment, a relationship was taking shape, that active sharing between child and therapist was an essential dimension of relationship—the therapist's theories, ideas, thoughts, feelings, and preferences enter into interactions with children.

As relationship therapy became the model and guide for my work with children, I studied Otto Rank's *Will Therapy and Truth and Reality* (1936) and Jessie Taft's *The Dynamics of Therapy in a Controlled Relationship* (1933).

In many ways, Taft's work with children provided the guides for establishing a therapeutic relationship. She advocated a process and procedures that emphasized the importance of waiting for a child to activate her or his powers and to direct the constructions of play within the child–therapist relationship. I worked with children extensively from 1949 to 1959. Over this ten-year period, I increasingly saw the value of Taft's commitment to the child and the significance of patience in relationship therapy.

Values and Attitudes of the Therapist

In the six years following publication of *Children in Play Therapy* (1953), I explored further the core attitudes of the therapist and how they enter into life with a child. In *Psychotherapy with Children* (1959), I described the heart of the child–therapist relationship—what it is and what it means. I emphasized that the therapist waits for the child, serves the child with patience and dedication, until the child is ready to face issues and challenges of living in accordance with her or his own nature. Waiting expresses the therapist's faith in the child's powers to be and to grow. The child is regarded as a person of distinctiveness and integrity. Again and again, I saw that the relationship between child and therapist facilitates freedom of expression, that through the relationship the child discovers and affirms a real self. Through the relationship, the child comes to value herself or himself, to affirm interests, thoughts, feelings, and internal directions that serve as guides to identity, self-expression, and self-understanding. The therapist, throughout the process, is *there* in the child's world, focusing directly on his or her feelings, thoughts, and wishes, responding as a person and in a way that encourages his or her explorations of self and others. In relationship therapy, the therapist participates in the child's plans, sometimes actively playing with the child on the child's invitation. The therapist also may facilitate a new growth direction through comments, guidelines, suggestions, always with respect for the child, listening with tenderness and concern, determined to understand the child's own perceptions and declarations of reality.

In *Psychotherapy with Children*, I emphasized that "the therapist begins where the child actually is and deals directly and immediately with the child's feelings rather than with his [or her] symptoms or problems. The therapist conveys his [or her] unqualified acceptance, respect, and faith in the child and the child's potentialities" (p. 5).

In every aspect of the relationship, the child is seen as an individual with an ever-present capacity for self-determination, a person who can make decisions that will contribute to self-fulfillment.

Self-abnegation, self-denial, a self withdrawn from or at war with the world is often at the root of a troubled child's way of being with others. Somewhere along the way, the child has given up the unique patterns that distinguish her or him from every other person. The growth of the self has been impaired often through criticism, ostracism, and rejection. The child has been cut off from vital self-resources that would enable him or her to develop in accordance with individual, personal talents. His or her behavior may seem inadequate or destructive to others. Only in a relationship in which the child is accepted and cherished as a lovable, whole person will he or she be able to recover a real self. The warm, compassionate empathy of an adult in relationship play therapy opens new visions and possibilities. The child is encouraged to talk freely, to make choices, to direct life and regain self-resources and self-esteem. Paradoxically, children who express hostility in play may become inwardly tranquil. In owning their fears, they may come to feel safe and unafraid. In admitting inadequacy, an inward openness may occur that makes possible an awakening of confidence and courage. Free to attack and destroy, children become free to love. Valid meanings exist only in the child's own perceptions of what is real.

In therapy, the child feels the complete, undivided attention of the adult, the concern and tender caring of the therapist. The child learns that regardless of the intensity or extremeness of the feelings, she or he will be accepted and encouraged to be. Such is the case in the play therapy session that follows.

Donald

Donald entered the playroom shaking, his body taut, tense, and constricted. He glared at me intently with an expression of anger on his face. After a few moments of silence, I spoke to him: "Children who come and play with me call me Mr. Clark. By what name shall I call you?"

"My father calls me Don but I want you to call me Donald and I will call you Clark" (*no change in the angry stare in my direction*).

At that, Donald moved quickly. I was momentarily stunned by the intensity, stiffness, and distortion of his body positioning.

"I'm going to get you," he almost silently whispered. "I'm going to cut you up in little pieces." He briefly examined and tested the medical instruments in the room. Leaving them, he grabbed a long sword, removed the protective covering and warned me, "I'm going to cut off your foot."

"I see you're determined to cut me up. I'll soon learn if I can take it. If you cut me gently perhaps that would be okay."

Donald proceeded to cut off my foot at the ankle. He continued, "Now I'll cut off your leg and your knee. I'll cut you good, there" (*pointing to my genital area*).

I stopped him saying, "That's not okay. That would hurt."

To my surprise, Donald readily accepted the limit and proceeded to cut off my stomach. "And now your heart." With the same intensity, he said, "Now your neck."

"You have cut me to pieces. There's nothing left of me."

"I have killed you."

In his fantasy world, and in the realities of play, Donald had completely eviscerated me. Every section of my body had been destroyed with an exaggerated violence.

"Donald, we have only about five minutes." His play shifted. The attacks had ended. We shared a wondrous silence. After about five minutes, I reached out to take his hand, saying softly, "Time to go." He accepted the time limit. We walked out of the play area, hand in hand, to meet his father.

Powers of Listening, Autonomy, and Will

Perhaps the most important attribute of the play therapist is his or her *presence* as a human being, a person committed to being with a child, listening and hearing the child's perceptions, thoughts, feelings, and meanings. Through empathy, compassion, and intuitive sensings, the therapist discerns the rhythms of the child, recognizes, accepts, and values the child's own ways, and reinforces the child's potentials for authentic expressions of self.

In my book *Who Will Listen?* (1975), the crucial nature of listening and hearing in relationship therapy is depicted:

> What does it mean to really know another person in significant moments of that person's life, to hear the range of voices, the variations of speech, the tones and textures, sounds of joy and anger, the mixture of sadness and laughter, the edgy, uncertain words of fear, the myriad facial and body expressions—surprise, doubt, shock, terror, rage, madness—the lengthy silences and continuous stream of words that seem never to stop coming, and all the ups and downs of ecstasy and misery?
>
> To fully know another person is a long journey of listening, feeling, sensing, risking, trusting, doubting, joining, wandering alone, fighting, loving, supporting, opposing, laughing, weeping. When two people actually meet and create a full life, a sense of mutuality is present, each is alive and responsive to the other. The vibrations are unlike any others. Such a relationship follows a unique path, without tangible or predictable directions, without prescribed rules and regulations. The essence of a living relationship is a mystery, happening but once and unrepeatable. The nature, substance, and character of a particular moment between two persons [are] unique and can never be replicated. [pp. xi–xii]

Many children, like Donald, from the first years of their lives have been repeatedly criticized, punished, negatively evaluated, restricted, and restrained. They have been isolated, scorned, and rejected. They have lost touch with inner stirrings of the heart. They dwell in subterranean places of the self, developing unusual competency in how to be defiant, resistant, silent. To reactivate a genuine self and the spirit of life may require prolonged affirmation, encouragement, and consistent expressions of caring from an adult. Unconditional support and love may awaken interior regions of the soul and move the child forward. This is a central goal of therapy—to reawaken the powers of self-direction and reactivate and strengthen the will, thus enabling children to find their own way.

As far back as my own early childhood, my belief in my own capacity to discover a way served me well in by-passing or overcoming barriers that others had erected on my path. My belief in my resources for transcending limits imposed by others was an unstoppable power. Every child that I have met in therapy over a period of forty-five years has benefited from my belief in her or him to find a way. Every child, through the consistent acceptance, respect, and faith of a play therapist, has in the process of therapy emboldened her or his will, exercised initiative, and become a self-starter.

The light of belief is transmitted from therapist to child. Everything else must wait. The being-there of child and therapist is a world light—steady, alive, present.

Limits in Relationship Therapy

Relationship therapy engenders freedom, choice, and self-direction. While freedom to be and to express oneself are constituents of effective play therapy, limits are also an essential ingredient. In *Psychotherapy with Children* (1959), I describe my view of limits:

> Without limits there could be no therapy. Limits define the boundaries of the relationship and tie it to reality. . . . They offer security and at the same time permit the child to move freely and safely in play. They help to make the playroom experience a living reality. [p. 10]

The will of the child is often severely tested in coping with limits, and in struggling to reconcile the therapist's encouragement of freedom and will with his or her setting of limits. There is a way to set and hold to limits while also affirming the child's expression of will and right to self-determination. Suggesting alternatives offers a possible solution for willful expression.

For example, in play therapy with Donald I recognized his obsession with cutting me into pieces. I accepted myself as his victim but I set a limit when he intended to cut into me with major force or when he wanted to cut off my genitals with a brandished sword. I am more reluctant to set limits when I am with children who are severely withdrawn, excessively polite, complacent, or placid, or

> [W]hen they readily turn over their fate to other children or adults, when the vital signs of impulse, energy, and spontaneity are dormant, when the will is so diminished that children fail to respond in a situation where anger and self-affirmation are valid protectors of the will. We should be concerned when a child's anger is cold, methodical, and devious. This often tells us that insidious and destructive tactics have been used to control a child, that the child's willfulness has been trampled on and impaired.
>
> Recognition of the will is a value of central importance. The struggle of the child is the struggle to remain an individual. In a sense, the real issue in all therapy is the battle of will, the chronicle of a person interfered with and crushed. Otto Rank (1936) has stated that ". . . the task of the therapist is not to act as will, which the patient would like, but only to function as counter-will in such a way that the will of the patient shall not be broken, but strengthened" (p. 16). [Moustakas 1981, pp. 75–76]

Setting and Meaning of Place

The setting in which play therapy occurs is determined to some degree by the presenting problem and by the age of the child. Gender also influences the way in which the child arranges the playroom and the materials chosen for play. Children often begin their play with items that are not clearly defined, such as paints, sand, clay, or water. Following exploration of "diffuse" items, children may choose trucks, cars, games, and books. The progression sometimes moves from sand to toys to family figures (typically, parents and siblings), and then to community figures (postal, fire, police, business, and other people).

To illustrate, I met with Tommy, 4 years old, shortly after his parents had adopted a 13-year-old girl and his mother had given birth to a daughter. The two events precipitated a radical change in Tommy's behavior, both at home and in school. He changed from a contented, happy, outgoing child to being sulky, withdrawn, and, at times, destructive. During his first play therapy session, he played quietly and alone, using mainly airplanes and trucks for the entire hour. In the second session, he concentrated on the family figures. During the hour, he focused exclusively on himself and his siblings. He expressed his angry feelings toward his two new siblings. Through the accepting and clarifying reflections of the therapist and through the play media, Tommy explored his feelings and ultimately began to see the benefits of a life with siblings.

In *Rhythms, Rituals, and Relationships* (1981), I emphasized that

[E]ven before a therapeutic relation begins, the therapist is aware of the importance of the place of the meetings, and the significance of what is generated by the setting and the arrangements. Four important dimensions of therapy are initially communicated through the climates we establish. The first challenge of the therapist is to create a therapy space and materials that are easily accessible. An atmosphere is created in which there is a definite sense of openness. The therapist offers a receptive and welcoming presence that encourages the child to experiment and explore, that invites the child to direct and take charge of her or his world.

The second challenge of the therapist is to create an atmosphere of freedom—to encourage the child to make choices, to decide on the basis of interest, desire, and attraction. The emotional climate conveys to the child: "This is your room—this is your time—create this world in your own way—arrange and rearrange this place as it suits you. You are in control of this environment. The power of life, the power of creation is within you. I am here to support you, to share this life, to be with you, to serve you in the ways that you choose to be and to grow."

The third challenge of the therapist is to establish an atmosphere of tranquility. To some degree this atmosphere is developed in the consistency of space, time, materials, and therapist behavior. An atmosphere of privacy is deliberately communicated to the child, a feeling of security, a sense that nothing confidential will be repeated, that there will be no betrayals, that the child's expressions and sharings are a sacred trust and remain sealed in the moment.

The fourth critical dimension of atmosphere is the communication of caring. From the start the therapist, in body language and words, conveys a clear and definite concern, an unwavering interest in the child's well-being. [pp. 59–60]

Number of Sessions

In relationship therapy, the child determines the length of time and number of sessions needed to come to terms with issues and problems of living connected with self, others, home, or school. Situational therapy is a brief therapy. It is effective when a child faces a temporary crisis—the birth of a sibling, move of a family residence, change of school, physical illness, or any temporary disturbance or distress.

Children direct the life of therapy and the length of time in therapy in accordance with their own purpose, vision, and destiny. Realities of child growth and development are to a significant degree shaped by internal processes of desire, motivation, and interest. When external rules and pressures dictate, something essential is lost in authenticity and timeliness, in the child's self-determination and self-affirmation, and in the knowledge which comes from one's own guides and directions.

Diagnosis and Assessment

Diagnoses, cause–effect inferences, manipulations and controls, predetermined and directed by the therapist, undermine the tenets, values, and meanings inherent in relationship therapy. They also ignore the values of immediacy, here-and-now perceptions, and the freedom to be and to direct one's own life. What matters is not what is derived from a cause–effect analysis, but how a child views life, what directs life in play therapy, what unique attributes and possibilities emerge as therapist and child meet person-to-person. What matters is the therapist's unqualified acceptance, understanding, and affirmation of the child's expressions of self. When assessments are made in relationship therapy, they are not based on diagnosis or a predetermined portrait of a child's condition, or a shrewd discernment of the child's symptoms. They are derived from the child's actual presentation of self in play therapy, his or her language, silences, choices, the way she or he structures the play materials, and the content projections of the play with reference to self and other. Thus, the focus of relationship play therapy is on who the child is in interactions with the therapist, the living relationship between child and adult, the natural, organic unfoldings of mutual experiences.

Parents and Families

Values of play therapy can be learned and applied by parents. From the beginnings of my work as a professional play therapist, I frequently held meetings with all of the parents whose children were enrolled at The Merrill-Palmer Institute. I also met with entire families, such as Kathy's family, described in Chapter 7. Many years later, Kathy contacted me and reviewed with me the nature of the family play therapy experience. Specifically, she commented on her relationship with her father. The play therapy had moved Kathy from intense anxiety when she was alone with her father, to feelings of comfort and ease, and finally to an open and trusting relationship with him.

My inclusion of parents in play therapy often resulted in their transferring their new-found knowledge and skills to interactions with members of their families of origin and with teachers in their children's schools. Sometimes parents confronted their own parents with residuals of childhood experiences in which they had felt controlled, misunderstood, and manipulated. Typically, these confrontations opened more natural, richer communications and relationships.

At times in my work with parents, I have suggested group therapy. For example, as I was meeting with Roy, Mike, and Barry in group play therapy, I also met with their parents, each of whom was extremely critical of their children's teachers and schools. The account of my work with children and families has been presented in detail in *Who Will Listen?* (1975).

Roy's, Barry's, and Mike's mothers entered therapy with me individually and as a group, initially as an outcome of conflicts with school personnel. They held teachers responsible for their children's antipathy toward, and failures in, school. Early in the meetings, the parents shifted from a focus on the children to a focus on the teachers, and then to a concentration on themselves and on their own parents.

Over the years, I have come to be convinced that family therapy works best when it grows out of the choices and needs of the individual children who are in therapy and when it is accepted and supported by the children. Typically, I have begun my work with a child following a preliminary meeting with the parents. After the initial meeting with parents, I meet the child for three or four play therapy sessions. Then the child, parents, and I would meet to discuss the core themes and directions of the play therapy and to develop a plan for continuing the work. Such a plan often leads to parents, and sometimes siblings, joining the child in some of the play therapy sessions. However, throughout my work with children, I always consider the individual child my primary commitment. Sibling therapy and family therapy, when the conditions are congruent with the well-being of the individual child and the tenets of relationship therapy, facilitate, strengthen, and serve as catalysts, in the process of the child's recovery of his or her powers and authentic ways of being.

Parent education and training is an important aspect of work with children in play therapy. Through such training, parents learn much more about their children, what and how they feel and think, who they are. Play is the natural means of child expression and offers parents an ideal way of advancing an understanding of their children. Play presents opportunities for parents to enter their children's worlds and learn what is essential to them. It invites parents to convey their valuing of their child, and their acceptance, support, and understanding of her or him. Children's play holds meanings; the parent–child relationship is enhanced when parents recognize these meanings. In many instances of work with children at a standstill, my most significant breakthroughs occurred when parents joined me with their child in the playroom. They were able to observe directly my communications and interactions with their child and later to discuss with me ways of promoting their child's creative growth. They were able to recognize the unique resources and talents of their child, and affirm their child's identity.

Educating and Training Students

Looking back over these many years of involvement with children and families in play therapy, and looking toward the education and training of students wanting to become effective play therapists, certain visions, beliefs, and knowledge stand out. What would I suggest to individuals responsible for educating and training students in play therapy? What would I offer students who desire to work with children—all children—but particularly those who are viewed as problems by their parents, teachers, or society?

On the way to becoming a play therapist, one must understand oneself, one's own beliefs, attitudes, values, the qualities of one's being, the nature of one's life, one's internal proclivities, resources, and tendencies, and external talents and skills. To know oneself in truth and fully is the direct path to being receptive to and knowing others.

The would-be play therapist must have an unyielding belief in the child and respect his or her choices, decisions, and powers of self-determination and self-direction—no matter how disturbed, troubled, or apparently limited the child.

From experiences of unconditional caring for and receptiveness to children, knowledge of theories of personality, child development, the psychology of adjustment, and psychopathology, students have the initial scholarly background to begin to concentrate on the practice of play therapy. Such a background should be supplemented by extensive observations of children and interactions with children, parents, and families.

Beginners in play therapy should videotape their interviews and study the film and transcriptions. They should witness directly what children say, how the therapist responds, and the impact on the relationship. Group play therapy is also an important part of a sequence of training challenges, as is family play therapy.

Studies of key play therapy references, immersions into the world of childhood, conversations with children in play, and talks with parents contribute to the knowledge, competencies, and skills needed to become a play therapist.

The Being of the Play Therapist

Perhaps what is most essential is the *being* of the play therapist. This registers in openness and receptiveness to child life. The therapist must love children, enjoy playing with children, and be able to enter the child's world and learn directly from his or her unfolding processes and directions in play.

This passage from *Who Will Listen?* (1975) further clarifies the meaning of relationship therapy, capturing the essence of the play therapist's life with children.

Knowing the other person and knowing myself with that person, living the relationship in a full and complete way, creating a unique and incomparable pattern of experience—these are the basic challenges of my encounters with children and parents in therapy. I have attempted to portray some of these challenges in the process of their creation and to point positively to the uniqueness, the unpredictability, and the mystery of human engagement. Each moment with another human being represents an opportunity for discovery and birth, or for confusion and destruction. Each moment holds the potential for life and death. I have chosen to live and to infuse my spirit into each human venture, to risk my own self in the hope of knowing the glory of a voice that speaks for the first time, of recognizing the birth of individuality, of seeing dead energy and spirit suddenly emerging into new forms and activities and sparking a light that grows from darkness. [p. xii]

2

Attitudes and Processes in Play Therapy

*F*or many years, administrative work and university teaching prevented me from doing play therapy. Recently play therapy entered my life again. Visions of children appear in my reflections, in the pictures in my mind, in virtually every region of my life. I am in touch with human values, techniques, tools, and methods that pervade the relationship in play therapy and determine therapeutic outcomes.

Child-centered therapists particularly understand the nature and meaning of play. They have worked successfully with emotionally disturbed children, with children diagnosed as physically handicapped or mentally retarded, and with children coping with reading and other school problems, or facing temporary losses or major life transitions. Play therapists have met with teachers and parents, attempting to help them develop a compassionate understanding of children, and ways to respond to them effectively.

Fixation on therapist techniques stops real exploration of relationships with children in therapy. What matters are the values and attitudes of the therapist—*respect* for the child, *acceptance* of the child's silent and verbal expressions, and *faith* in the child's unique potentials for directing his or her life.

The Therapist's Attitudes

The therapist's attitudes create a climate and structure in and through which children are invited to express themselves fully, in their own way, so that eventually they may achieve feelings of security, adequacy, and worthiness. Such feelings cannot be taught directly but can be created in the climate of play therapy and be transmitted from therapist to child.

Faith

There is no clear-cut formula by which a therapist conveys faith in children, acceptance of their creations, and respect. Faith in children is essential to their emotional organization and growth. Faith is an intangible quality, perceived largely through the presence of feelings and body positions and expressions. It generates energy and inspiration in and between therapist and child. When someone has faith in us, we are encouraged to face ourselves and express ourselves and grow in terms of the persons we really are.

Faith is expressed in both subtle and direct ways. Children sense others' faith in them. They are able to describe the feeling as an essential quality of the relationship. Axline (1950) long ago offered these vivid expressions of the meaning of faith:

> . . . you were the first person who ever believed in me—who didn't think I was all bad—who didn't think I was silly—who took the time to try to find out how I felt about things. [p. 59]
>
> I think this all happened to me because you gave me a chance to believe in *me*. And then I felt I *was* worthwhile. . . . As I think back about it you didn't seem to do a thing but be there. And yet a harbor doesn't do anything either, except to stand there quietly with arms always outstretched waiting for the travellers to come home. I came home to myself through you. [p. 60]

Children who believe in themselves are able to make decisions with conviction, and carry out actions with confidence. Children who experience faith in themselves know what they want to do, what they can do, and what they will do. They trust their own feelings and choices.

The therapist who has faith in the child sometimes conveys this in simple expressions. "That's entirely up to you," "You're the best judge of that," or "What is important is your own decision, what you want to do." In faith, the therapist conveys a genuine belief that children have within themselves the capacity for growth and self-realization.

Acceptance

Acceptance is a less elusive quality than faith. It is more clearly differentiated and better understood. Acceptance is not mere acquiescence. It is not a passive process, nor is it a noncommittal attitude. Acceptance involves a real commitment on the part of the therapist, a nonjudgmental feeling, a valuing, expressed directly to the child, in alive interactions between child and therapist. In these interactions, the child feels understood. Personal meanings are affirmed and supported.

To different children, objects have different meanings. Sand, clay, water, and paints offer many possibilities for exploring feelings that involve parents and siblings—anger, fear, love, hate, sadness, and hostility. In imaginative play and in fantasy, the therapist follows the child's leads, offering various objects, such as cars, knives, soldiers, guns, boats and other play things, to encourage and support play creations. The therapist, in words and silences, accepts the child's symbolic shapings and formings exactly as conveyed.

The relationship play therapist indicates acceptance through various expressions such as: "Mm-hm," "I see," "That's the way you feel," "You're really afraid of him," "I understand what it means to you," "What do you see it as?" Through words, silences, and tacit feelings, the therapist facilitates a therapeutic relationship with a child. The relationship is the heart and soul of play therapy.

Acceptance is undermined when a therapist criticizes children or rewards them and approves of their behavior. Children who are rewarded tend to direct their actions to whatever brings favor and avoid what they have learned will be rejected.

Respect

Closely allied to faith and acceptance is the therapist's communication of respect. Children who feel respected feel that their interests are understood and valued, that the therapist is concerned about them as persons. Respect is conveyed in the way the therapist greets a child and responds to his or her words, silences, and play creations.

In conveying respect, a therapist recognizes that children have the right to their feelings and thoughts. The therapist does not interpret a child's words and silences, or divert from, ignore, or deny their presence. The message he or she conveys is, "Your words and feelings are part of you; I honor them as I do all aspects of your self." The play therapist affirms whatever a child reveals, whatever is expressed, whatever is a facet of the child's personality. Of itself, every expression of the child is of value in relationship therapy.

The relationship play therapist respects children's habits and mannerisms, and does not attempt to change children or persuade them to modify their behavior to satisfy others' standards. The therapist who respects children believes that all children have potentialities for self-direction and effective decision making.

Unity of the Therapist's Attitudes

Faith, acceptance, and respect are intimately bound together in the therapeutic relationship. Faith is expressed in the belief that a child holds the key and the resources for working out difficulties and for discovering what is best. Acceptance is conveyed when the therapist encourages children to express their feelings and explore their attitudes freely. Respect in relationship therapy means that children are received in their own style and ways, that who they are and what they say is worthwhile and worthy of positive attention and response.

In relationship therapy, play therapists are present as persons. They are aware, moment by moment, of the values of faith, acceptance, and respect as living realities in the social-emotional climate of play therapy.

The Therapeutic Process

In relationship therapy, the therapeutic process follows a consistent pattern: as therapy begins, the emotional expressions in disturbed and troubled children are diffuse and undifferentiated. Typically, these children have lost touch with people and situations that originally aroused frustration, anger, fear, or guilt. Their emotions are no longer tied to the realities of everyday living; they are magnified, generalized, easily stimulated and evoked.

Unfocused Negative Feelings

Hostility, anxiety, and regression pervade disturbed children's expressions in play therapy. Fear and anger often are unfocused, not directed toward particular persons or emotional experiences. Many children enter play therapy afraid of almost everything, wanting to destroy the people figures, or they wish to be silent and left completely alone.

Anger is often expressed in direct attacks on people figures and other toys—smashing, pounding, breaking, tearing, crushing, and strangling. These attacks may appear to be without purpose. Nothing in the therapy relationship appears to provoke the intense feelings that launch the play therapy process. The level of trust, to a great degree, determines the nature and quality of the feelings that may be safely expressed. When the child feels accepted and respected, a sense of power and confidence awakens that facilitates expressions of anger, pain, or sorrow.

Clarifying Negative Feelings

As the relationship between child and therapist is clarified and strengthened, the child's feelings are sharpened and become more specific. Often they are directed toward particular persons—parents, siblings, an entire family. Pounding, smashing, and expressions of the desire to kill are not uncommon in play therapy.

As children express and release more and more of their negative feelings in direct ways toward the people in their lives who have undermined them, and as these expressions are accepted by the therapist, the feelings become less intense and have less power over the child. Anger, for example, becomes mixed with caring. Ambivalence toward particular people registers in the child's play activities. The child's anger toward a baby brother or sister may fluctuate in the play, as the child feeds and protects the baby and then suddenly spanks him or her. Negative feelings may be intense at first, but as they are expressed again and again in an accepting therapeutic relationship, they become less forceful. In the final stage of this process, positive feelings begin to strengthen. Children see themselves more as they really are. They may still resent a sibling but typically positive feelings dominate. As one 4-year-old expressed in one of her final sessions, "I'm going to have a big party and invite everybody, even my baby brother."

The resolution of negative feelings such as anger may be summarized as follows: First, anger is diffuse and pervasive. Next, it becomes focused and directed, typically toward parents, siblings, other children, the therapist, relatives, or other significant people in the child's life. The negative anger remains specific but is mixed with positive feelings. Finally, positive and negative feelings are separated and more consistent with the realities that motivate them. The intensity of feelings accompanying these stages also seems to change. In the beginning, negative feelings of anger are severe. During the therapeutic process, they become less intense. Finally, they become moderate in children's play expressions.

In the beginning of relationship therapy, anxiety also is commonly diffuse. The child is withdrawn and frightened, tense and garrulous, sometimes over-anxious about being clean, neat, or orderly. Anxiety immobilizes children. They have difficulty starting anything, or completing anything. In anxiety, children do not know how to go about doing what they really want to do. Their anxious fears take many forms—night terrors, bizarre fears of animals and things, terrors of the unseen, of movements, sounds, and visions. Anxiety becomes an obsession. As relationship therapy unfolds, the anxiety focuses on specific fears—fears of one's father or mother or some other particular person or thing. During the therapeutic process, fear shifts toward confidence, threat toward courage. The feelings are clearer and more in line with the actual situations that evoke them.

The negative and positive feeling tones and the shifts that occur in children's play are not distinct entities or even always distinctly observable. They emerge and become transformed, not step by step, but in individually varying sequences. They overlap at many points, yet there are typical sequences of the play therapy process.

The following is an example (taken from tape-recorded interviews and stenographic notes) of a 7-year-old girl in relationship play therapy.

Karen

In the hours of play therapy with Karen and in talks with her parents, the world in which Karen lived gradually emerged. In this world, three centers of pressure converged to create feelings of helplessness and terror. The severest of these pressures was the daily climate of threat in the classroom and particularly in Karen's contacts with her first-grade teacher. Out of the meetings with Karen, a pattern of her school life emerged, reflected in the following incident, which Karen described in one of our conversations.

> Mrs. Brooks was always yelling and getting mad at us. When she jumped on Peter she scared me. Peter sat next to me in school and she came screaming at him. Her face was ugly. She shook him and shouted, "Peter, I told you to listen when I pronounce the words, didn't I? You aren't listening, are you, Peter? You're stupid! You belong in kindergarten with the other babies. There is no place for you; you're wasting our time. Now go put your face against the wall for the rest of the reading period."

In school, Karen often lived in a state of fear. She was an extremely sensitive, caring person, and on this day, she experienced Peter's shame as her own. She felt his humiliation as a shock to her own existence.

Each morning as Karen got ready for school, she would feel a vague, violent dread, cumulative and unrelenting. The fear was present when she awoke in the morning. It grew into terror as Karen imagined the consequences of being the next victim of her teacher's angry outbursts. Only with much effort and strain could she bring herself to leave her home and take the steps that would bring her to the doors of the school. Increasingly, Karen found it difficult to concentrate, to listen, and to relate to others. She became convinced that she was stupid and that one day she would make a mistake that would cause her teacher to spring upon her. Many times as she watched others suffer, she felt their pain.

The teacher's use of corporal punishment, constant threat (both implied and stated), and belittlement and sarcasm frightened Karen. Karen had good reason to fear her teacher, although her experience of this fear was enlarged beyond the bounds of what was happening in school.

In her concern for others, Karen absorbed an enlarged grief. Each time she witnessed brutality, each time she saw the distorted faces and shaking bodies, she cringed a little more. She came to feel that she was guilty. She saw herself on trial for each classroom misdemeanor. Every act of stupidity was her stupidity. Every blunder was her mistake. She had the strong feeling that the eyes of her teacher were always watching her, judging her, and waiting for the proper moment to punish her. Increasingly, her world tightened. She was convinced that she was doomed to suffer a severe punishment. It was only a matter of time.

Karen wanted to escape. She wanted to run away. Yet each day she came to school, reluctantly and filled with increasing fear. She saw no exit, no way out of her awful predicament, no escape from the inevitable accusation and punishment. In her imaginings and fantasies, she began to create macabre tales, and out of them grew a new form of terror—waking, screaming, and shaking uncontrollably in the middle of her nightmares.

In addition to the fears and the nightmares, Karen began to experience physical illness—nausea, and dizziness in and on the way to school.

She felt she was under surveillance, that she was being critically inspected, and the terror of this feeling spread until she was afraid to speak of it at all. She remained quiet at school, frozen in a private world of enormous fear.

The second center of pressure that Karen faced daily occurred at home. She tried to talk with her parents, to tell them that she was afraid of her teacher—terribly, terribly afraid. But they would not listen. They thought she complained unnecessarily and that her stories were exaggerated. When she complained of illness in the morning, they would not permit her to remain at home. The nightmares bothered them but only enough to control the kinds of programs she watched on television. She was forced to continue in a school situation where she felt increasingly disabled and defenseless. She felt her parents did not understand or support her. She began to slip away from life at home and at school into a world of frightening images, of ghosts and witches, of knives and blood and broken bones.

When the tension reached an unbearable point, what Karen had feared most happened. Mrs. Brooks saw that "something strange was happening to Karen" but she did not know what or why. I have paraphrased Mrs. Brooks's description of the moment and Karen's retelling of it into one account of the day Karen's world crashed in on her.

Mrs. Brooks was explaining a lesson in the workbook. Suddenly she stopped. Her eyes focused tightly on Karen. She took several steps toward her. Their eyes met for a moment. Karen stood up. Her entire body stretched. Her arms extended upward and a look of absolute alarm passed across her face. She began spinning and spinning until each item, each person in the room revolved with her. This was it. The grave moment had come. She was experiencing an all-encompassing panic. Just as her teacher reached her, Karen lost consciousness. She slumped over her desk, making weird, grotesque, agitated body movements, convulsive motions of her muscles. She was having a brain seizure.

Karen was taken to a nearby children's hospital for a complete analysis of the convulsive disorder. Thorough laboratory and medical tests over a two-day hospitalization revealed completely negative results. There was no physical basis for the convulsion. The physician con-

cluded that it was caused by extreme muscular tension which he believed had been induced by psychic tensions and fears. He recom-
mended that Karen not return to the public school and referred her
parents to me.

At last, Karen's parents realized that her fear of school had a basis
in reality. They knew now that they had contributed to her illness by
not listening to her, by not being sympathetic and supportive when she
tried to express her extreme reactions to school. They had thought that
her physical complaints were dramatic gestures for getting attention and
attempts to evade school. They had not understood the grave crisis
Karen faced. They had not been a part of her private world of thought
and feeling simply because they were too involved in their own expectations and goals. Once they understood, they decided to seek appropriate help for themselves and for Karen. They realized that Karen had
become a stranger to them. They wanted to know her real feelings and
perceptions, to understand her in her own unique selfhood.

The third center of pressure in Karen's world was her neighborhood. Her parents were in conflict with neighborhood ethics and prac-
tices. They held to principles of individual rights and peaceful group
life, and attempted to inculcate these standards and values in their daily
living in the family. Karen lived in a segregated community on the fringe
of the city in a marginal area where homes were substandard and rapidly disintegrating. It was an unstable, transient community, with a
congested population and extremely limited space. There were no
parks, playgrounds, or recreational areas in the immediate vicinity. The
delinquency rate was high. Fighting in the streets, loud night quarrels,
and battles with the police were frequent occurrences. Karen had witnessed knife fights. Other children tried to provoke her into fighting.
Some brandished knives before her and threatened her. She would run
into her house and withdraw for hours in silent isolation. On one occasion, she saw a child in front of her house covered with blood and being
taken away by an ambulance. She could still hear the shrill sirens. The
sights and sounds terrified her. Karen herself was a pacifist, verbalizing her conviction that fighting was wrong and could only harm people.
She often asked why people could not live peacefully, why they wanted

to hurt each other, why they hated rather than loved each other. Her extremely sensitive ways and her acute perceptiveness brought her daily anguish and unhappiness.

Karen's Conversations with Her Father

Since there was a delay in Karen's initial meeting with her therapist, her father, an elementary school teacher, decided to attempt a new approach with her. He studied a number of books on child guidance, took a graduate course in methods of counseling, and discussed therapeutic procedures with his wife. He began, in a simple way, to apply therapeutic principles and procedures in some of his contacts with Karen. Each day, he reserved a period of time to be alone with her. At these times, he gave Karen his complete attention. He encouraged her to express her feelings and to share with him her wishes and fears, her hopes and desires, her interests and attitudes. Following these meetings, he sat quietly by himself thinking through the moments with her, recapturing their conversations, attempting to understand the nature and meaning of Karen's existence. He kept a journal of some of these conversations. Several excerpts convey the nature of the new, developing relationship between Karen and her father.

On one occasion, as Karen's father sat nearby while she bathed, the following conversation took place:

> K: I'm going to tell you a secret. I might as well tell you, Daddy. (*Pause.*) I've got a secret. When you put me to bed, sometimes you spank me. I laugh. I wait until you're gone. When I know you're downstairs, then I laugh.
> F: Like this: HA! HA! HA!
> K: Just laugh. You don't hurt me.
> F: Funny daddy.
> K: Yeah.
> F: You know I never mean to hurt you.
> K: Yeah, I know.

On another occasion, Karen and her father came into conflict over her bedtime. An argument had been underway for several minutes when Karen began to cry. In a highly emotional voice, she protested the inconsistency between her parents and referred to her mother's promise.

K: Mother said I could stay and watch until I got tired. And now you say I can't.

F: When is that? How long do you want to watch?

K: Until I get tired.

F: That's just what you said before, until you got tired. I don't think that's a good idea.

K: But Mommy promised. And now you say . . . (*cries violently*).

F: I know, but Mommy and I never discussed this. You can go watch TV but if you don't decide to go to bed at a reasonable time, then . . .

K: How long?

F: You watch until I come down unless you tire before then. But when I come downstairs, I'm going to say, "Karen, you're going to bed now" and that's that! Do you understand?

K: Yes. (*After about half an hour, Karen, on her own, approaches her father.*) Daddy, I'm getting tired now. See my eyes, they're sleepy, aren't they?

F: Yes. You're ready. Up we go. (*Karen kisses her father.*) I'm so glad I have you.

K: M-m-m.

F: I love you when you're bad and I love . . .

K: Love me when I'm good. (*Father takes Karen up to bed.*)

In another meeting with her father, Karen explores her troubled feelings.

F: You look so unhappy, Karen. What's the matter?

K: I don't know.

F: Why don't you like yourself? Why don't you like Karen? (*Long pause.*)

K: I'm so dumb.

F: You? Dumb?

K: Yeah. I can't read.

F: (*Emphatically*) You are not dumb and you read well. (*Long pause.*)

K: I'm so . . . (*Pause.*)

F: So . . . what?

K: In . . . con, I can't pronounce it.

F: Inconsiderate?

K: Yes, inconsiderate to everyone.

F: Karen, you are not dumb. You read as well as most children. And you love us and we love you . . . and even if you were dumb or inconsiderate, which you are not, I'd still love you.

K: Daddy, I love you, too.

In this final excerpt, Karen and her father are lying side by side. They have been together for a long while. Then as Karen looks out the window she begins to speak.

K: I'm looking at the trees. They teach people a lesson.

F: What do they teach you, Karen?

K: The leaves are their lips and with their branches they look up to God and God sees them and helps them.

F: Where did you learn that, Karen?

K: I don't know. (*Pause.*) Ride me downstairs now.

F: Okay.

These private meetings between Karen and her father paved the way for the therapy that followed. In these meetings, a process had begun in which Karen became increasingly open with her parents. A climate was created in which her parents shared her struggle to learn to live with herself in a threatening world. A pattern of relating was evolving in which the individuality and uniqueness of Karen and her need for recognition were valued and given opportunity for expression.

Relationship Play Therapy

Even so, Karen was still an easily frightened child. When she arrived for her first hour of therapy, she was withdrawn and evasive. She needed to be reassured again and again that in the playroom she was free to do what she wanted. She needed to be supported to make decisions that made sense to her. It was necessary to reaffirm that the toys and materials were there for her and that no one would interrupt us. Slowly, she came to realize that I was to be with her, to listen to and speak to her, to enable her to face her conflicts and fears, and to express herself openly. It was obviously a new situation for Karen, a situation in which she did not need to seek attention and recognition because an adult was always present and attentive to her.

She entered for the first time in a quiet, frightened way, a stranger in a new setting, suspicious and distrustful. She looked around the room, evading me, and seeking a spot in a corner of the sandbox. With her back to me, she slowly began to finger the sand. She remained in this way for the entire hour, afraid to face me, afraid to face the situation, restricting herself to the sandbox, and to idle movements that seemed to comfort her. Only once did she look in my direction and then but fleetingly. Obviously, Karen needed more time to take the first step toward an expanding self, more time to overcome the fear of the stranger in herself and the stranger in me. By the end of the session there was one definite, observable change. The tension in her body disappeared; the agony of the beginning minutes was gone; Karen was relaxed throughout her body.

So our first hour came to a close with only one moment of direct communication between us. Somehow the silence we shared was not unpleasant or without meaning. As Karen left, her eyes were smiling; the therapy had registered. The quiet, serene atmosphere, the patient waiting, the adult's concern and constant presence, the freedom engendered, were all beginning to create a structure, a climate in which Karen could discover new regions within herself, new directions to enrich her life with others, and new resources for realizing her potentialities. The vast silence we shared in this hour was a way of living, a peaceful way, which Karen had not often known. My respect for her and her readiness for a new life, her way of emerging in accordance with her own timetable, gave her the conditions she needed to explore her world and to develop more fully as a real self.

So I waited for Karen to act. I waited for her to make decisions. I waited for her to take the first step toward a new life. When it happened, the shift was not a slow, gradual process but rather sudden and dramatic. Once she understood the nature of our meetings, once she internalized the values involved within the consistent structure of relationship therapy, Karen began to trust, to be spontaneous, to express and explore her world, and to share this expanding world with me.

In the second interview, the range of activity spread as did her use of the toys and materials. She initiated conversations with me. At one point, she spilled water on the floor and seemed considerably upset. She looked at me and waited for the criticism or punishment. When I made no comment, she hurried to get a sponge and wipe it up. I told her, "In here if you spill and mess, it is all right. . . . As long as you don't mind, it doesn't bother me."

Karen returned to the sandbox, mixing sand and water. Drops of water spilled on the floor. Momentarily, she looked in my direction, then she continued her play. She spilled a little of the wet sand on her dress. She looked at me and suddenly began to laugh, loudly.

CM: In here you can laugh about messing. But what about at home?
 K: No, there I have to keep clean. When I play with mud, I keep away from my mother. I try to wash it off before she sees me but sometimes she catches me and screams "K-A-R-E-N!"
CM: So, at home there are some things your mother doesn't like you to do?
 K: Yes, many things.
CM: You are not always free to do what you want to do.
 K: No. Not free.

Karen really came to life as she talked of her relationship with her mother. Enthusiastically, she stirred water into the sand, mixed it, and sang: "Lots of water, loads of sand, first sand, then water. Scoop it and scoop it many different ways. But only one way to get dirty. Only one way. Dirty is dirty. Look, now you are a mess. And I don't care. Here we go again."

Later in the interview while punching "Bobo," Karen began to talk in a low voice.

> K: I punch you some more. (*Punches silently several times.*) You are not fast enough. You are too slow. (*The punching becomes harder, more frenzied.*) Again and again I tell you. You don't do what I say. (*The punching continues. Karen is conversing with Bobo.*) You don't listen to me. You better pay attention. You'll see. You'll see.

The conversations continued to the end of the hour. As she played, Karen described in detail her school experience of the previous year. It was obvious that there was a strong residue of feeling against her public school teacher but, after a lengthy expression of feelings, after relating the incidents leading up to the final collapse and removal from school, she could sympathize with Mrs. Brooks: "Mrs. Brooks had forty-three children to teach and that's a big job." "Sometimes we wouldn't listen to her and she had a right to be mad at us." "I don't believe she wanted to hurt me or anyone. She wanted to frighten us so we would learn."

Change of School

Shortly after Karen began therapy, a plan was evolved with her parents to place her in a private school where pressures for academic achievement were at a minimum, where she would be a member of a small group in which individual differences were respected, where she could develop skills and knowledge at her own pace. The private school turned out to be an ideal placement in which Karen created a new image of teachers and schools. Within six weeks, she had developed a new concept of herself in school. She became confident in her reading and arithmetic abilities. Her achievement was much higher than that of any other child in her group. She became an assistant to the teacher—her unusual sensitivity, her wish to help, and her understanding that learning can be difficult and painful enabled her to assist other children to increased knowledge and skill and to new attitudes about themselves as learners.

One excerpt illustrates the meaningful nature of Karen's relationship with the play materials.

Karen procured a large piece of wood and several tools. She began to saw the wood.

K: Oh, wood! Oh, wood! How you hurt when I saw you. But I'll make you into something new and something good. (*She continues to talk in this way until she saws the board in half.*) Now I'll nail you together. Wait, this nail is going in crooked. Oh, I'll have to take you out. Now stand straight until I get you in. (*Pause. Tries again but fails.*) I'm losing my patience.

CM: But you don't want to quit.

K: No, but I'm losing my temper.

CM: Then you will be in a jam.

K: But I want to do it. Come on now. What's wrong? Is it you or is it me? (*Keeps working.*) There I got you. I got you right in. Ha! Ha! Ha! Ha! Now I'll put in your brother and see what happens.

Karen involved herself in a variety of self-chosen activities. She used clay to cook meals that she served to us. The meals were cooked her way, by her own recipes. She made this clear to me before serving. She often exclaimed, "This is fun. This is really fun." She spoke of the delicious pies, cakes, and jellies which her grandmother made for her, saying with an ecstatic look on her face, "I love her food!"

Sometimes she played with the family figures. Occasionally, she scolded them, spanked them, or isolated them in different parts of the room, as in the following sequence.

Karen takes a father, mother, sister, and baby figure. One by one she examines them. She twists the bodies, saying, "Look, I can twist these. Father is a big guy." She continues to twist the figures. She scolds each family member as she sets the father, mother, sister, and baby precariously on top of a wall of the playhouse. Then, she topples them over one by one. The "sister" begins to cry.

> K: She is crying. She is unhappy when they fight.
> CM: She doesn't like them to fight.
> K: No! Stop! Stop fighting!
> CM: She becomes very sad when they fight.
> K: They shouldn't fight. They shouldn't ever fight. They should always be friends.

As my meetings with Karen progressed, more and more she turned to painting and drawing and to reading books, either silently or aloud to me. There were occasions when she read silently or painted quietly for the entire hour. It was good just to be present with her, to see her completely relaxed and contented, to see her totally absorbed in activity, and finding joy in being involved.

Her drawings and paintings were generally nature scenes. She made "soft, white snow," "dancing clouds," and "fresh baby flowers." During these moments, Karen would occasionally sing or speak with me.

> K: These are fresh baby flowers, like in my garden.
> CM: Do you tend the flowers?
> K: Yes, I do. (*Pause. Karen sings as she paints.*)
> CM: You're in a happy mood today.
> K: Yeah. Everything is fine.
> CM: Not just here but at home.
> K: Yeah.
> CM: And at school.
> K: Yeah.
> CM: Everywhere.
> K: (*Smiles.*) Yes! Everywhere.

At the end of three months in her private school, Karen's parents moved. In discussions with her parents, it was decided to try Karen in the public school in her new neighborhood. This decision was discussed with Karen in one of our meetings.

> CM: Perhaps your parents have talked with you about going to a new school.
>
> K: Yes. They have.
>
> CM: They decided they wanted you to return to a public school so you would be more a part of your own neighborhood and go to school with the kids near your new home.
>
> K: Yes. I've seen the school. It's only a short way from where we live.
>
> CM: Are you ready to make a change, to leave your school? You know you can take as much time as you need to make the transfer.
>
> K: I visited there one day and met the teacher. She was nice to me. She invited me in and I sat by the window. I saw some beautiful trees through the window.
>
> CM: Perhaps it will be hard for you to change schools. You've been so happy where you are. (*Pause.*) Have you thought about when you would like to make a transfer? (*Long pause.*) Perhaps in a week or two?
>
> K: This week.
>
> CM: But there are only two days left.
>
> K: I'll tell my friends good-bye tomorrow.
>
> CM: Okay. I'll call Mr. Jensen, the principal of your new school, and see if you can begin on Friday. If not, perhaps you could start Monday morning. I'll call you at home tomorrow and let you know.
>
> K: Okay.

For the next ten minutes, Karen talked about school experiences, her teacher, and her friends. She related a number of enjoyable events and activities. There was a wistful, sad quality in her voice.

> CM: A little sad to leave your school.
>
> K: Yes. (*Long pause, then Karen painted silently the rest of the hour.*)

In our next meeting, Karen spoke at length about her new school. She had already initiated a number of friendships. Her teacher was kind to her, and she enjoyed the activities of the school. Obviously, from her own statements, she was positively launched in a new community. Three months later Karen brought her report card. She received four As and two Bs. It was shortly after this time that Karen decided to terminate the hours of therapy. Discussion with her parents confirmed my observation that for some months she had been growing in a spontaneous, creative way, developing her potentialities, establishing friendships, and broadening the scope of her interests and activities. The new neighborhood offered her a spacious world with expanded recreational and human resources.

3

Preventive Play Therapy

Many years ago, as a psychologist at the Merrill-Palmer Institute in Detroit, I met all children enrolled in the nursery school for play therapy. Every child was given an opportunity to express feelings and to work through problems in the play setting of relationship therapy. As part of this program, I also met with parents.

Parents' Involvement

At various times during the school year, I introduced individual parents and groups of parents to the philosophy, approaches, and techniques of relationship play therapy. These meetings provided parents with an opportunity to raise questions and examine communications and relationships with their children. Parents visited the playroom and were introduced to the play materials and the observation room. They were shown the microphones and recording machines. Methods of recording and transcribing play sessions were described. Excerpts from recordings or transcriptions were shared with parent groups. Parents were encouraged to discuss issues and concerns regarding their own family relationships.

Over the years, I have continued to include parents in discussion groups and invite them to join their children in play therapy sessions. Parents frequently ask questions about the nature of children's play and the meaning of play creations and their children's fantasy life.

They are interested in the play materials and their arrangement in the room. They want to know how children use the toys. They are curious about the therapist's interactions with children. They are especially interested in when and how limits are set and how they are maintained.

When parents understand play therapy and its outcomes, they become enthusiastic. They see the connection between emotional frustrations and disturbances in children and impaired family relationships. Many parents recognize that feelings of inferiority may arouse anger or fear, that the more severe the child's self-rejection, the more likely the child will experience self-alienation, anxiety, and hostility. Parents become aware, personally and intensely, that their own strong negative attitudes undermine their children's inner resources, and interfere with their thought processes and positive actions.

No matter how many mistakes parents have made, how insensitive and unresponsive they may have been in responding to children's interests, feelings, and choices, the possibility of reversing negative relationships between parents and children is always present. Supporting and affirming children and encouraging their expression and exploration of feelings are continuing challenges of relationship play therapy. Through the relationship, children learn to direct themselves toward creating joyful experiences with other children and adults.

First Contacts with the Child

All children experience frustration and tension that they cannot easily disclose at home or at school. All children have inner motivations which they will not reveal under ordinary circumstances.

In my contact with schools, teachers have sometimes requested that a child be seen in play therapy. Parents also have called me and referred their child for play therapy. Children enrolled at the Merrill-Palmer Institute invited themselves for play therapy. Typically I offered four play therapy sessions, whether the child was a self-referral, or referred by a teacher or parent.

Before coming to the playroom, the child is introduced to the therapist by the teacher or parent. The therapist sometimes observes the child in the home or school setting.

Valuing of the child and respect for the child's ability to make decisions are attitudes directly conveyed by the therapist in every contact with the child, including whether to participate in play therapy.

The Playroom and Materials

The playroom is a brightly colored, cheerful room. The materials are arranged in an unstructured fashion. No attempt is made to fix the identity of the toys or the contexts in which they are to be used. Trucks, cars, guns, knives, airplanes, sea divers, hot-water bottles, telephones, boats, and tractors are placed on shelves. Family and animal hand puppets, shovels, bowls, spoons, dolls, and a jump rope may also be found in the room. Crayons, clay, finger paint, paper, scissors, steel vises, tools, and plastic aprons are important items. A large dollhouse, doll furniture, and a number of doll figures are located in a corner of the room. In addition to these materials, the play therapy room includes nursing bottles, lead soldiers, sand, water, easel paints, masks, blocks, balloons, and a comeback toy (a large figure-like balloon weighted at the bottom).

The number of toys in the playroom is not of primary importance. What is important is that children not be pressured or forced into using the materials in any particular way. Children should feel free to project their own feelings onto the items in the playroom and use them, with few limits, in whatever way they choose.

Stability in Materials and Relationship

The materials and the relationship in play therapy remain stable. The play things are always arranged in the same way each time the child enters the room. The values and attitudes of the therapist remain constant, too. The materials and the relationship are the steady forces in relationship play therapy. Outside the playroom, the child lives in a changing world where others are often making the changes. In the playroom, the child is the decision maker and the guide.

As therapy progresses, the materials and the therapist's attitudes provide the resources for imaginative stories and dramatic creations that lead to a child's changing perceptions, understandings, and meanings. The faith, acceptance, respect, and caring of the therapist are sources of strength and security for the child, inspiring self-disclosure and pursuit of new possibilities for creation of value and meaning in play.

Structuring the Relationship

During the early phases of play therapy, structuring of the relationship is an essential process. It involves introducing the child to the playroom and creating a warm, permissive relationship. Through structuring, the therapist conveys attitudes of faith, acceptance, and respect. Structuring assists the child in gaining impressions of the nature and quality of the therapeutic relationship.

The therapist uses expressions, such as the following: "You may use the play things in any way that you want; I am not able to decide that for you; the important thing is that you choose for yourself and do what you want. You want me to name that for you but that's up to you. You want me to do that for you, but here you do things for yourself." Structuring the relationship and reinforcing the child's power to direct the life of the playroom allow the child to achieve a clear understanding of freedom and autonomy and to call upon her or his own powers to discover, explore, and actualize interests and potentials.

Reflection of Feelings

The primary purpose of reflecting feelings is to convey empathy to the child and to encourage the child to express his or her feelings. The empathic sharing of experiences reveals to children that their own ideas and feelings are what matter, that they are understandable and worthy. Reflections without acceptance, respect, and faith have little positive value in the child's world. The unfolding of therapeutic values depends on a close following of the child's feelings and thoughts and an understanding of the purpose and direction of a child's play.

Throughout relationship therapy, the therapist maintains a listening attitude. This means careful attention to the child's silent and verbal expressions and the content of the child's play. Therapeutic listening is a way of affirming every child's uniqueness and encouraging his or her disclosures and self-actualization.

Setting of Limits

An important responsibility of the play therapist involves the setting of limits. Limits connect the relationship to the realities of the everyday world. They define the boundaries of the relationship. They serve to remind children of their responsibilities to the therapist, the playroom, and to themselves.

A time limit is always set in play therapy, usually a 45-minute play period. The therapist indicates the time limit briefly, and alerts the child when only a few minutes remain at the end of the period, "I see that our time is almost up for today. We'll have to stop soon." Another limit involves the play materials. They must remain in the playroom. "I know you want to take that with you but it must remain here." Certain expensive or irreplaceable items may not be destroyed.

Realistically enough, the child is not permitted to physically abuse the therapist. "You really want to smear me with the paint, but that is one thing I will not allow you to do here."

Once a child decides to end a play session, the child may not come back into the playroom on that day. "You can go now if you want; it's up to you. If you leave, though, you will not be permitted to return today."

The boundaries of play therapy provide psychological limits and security, which act as a safeguard in the child's search for freedom.

Without these limits, children would move into situations that would unnecessarily or precipitously stimulate anxiety, arouse guilt, and create barriers in the relationship. In addition to the reality and security limits, health and safety limits also need to be set.

Other limits are set spontaneously, in the course of relationship play therapy. The therapist makes the distinction between permissiveness and practical reality. In most instances, children accept the limits but when a child ignores or rejects a limit, the therapist must decide what to do and how to reinforce the limit. While recognizing a child's feelings the therapist holds to the limit.

Through providing a stable, consistent environment, in structuring, reflecting, and setting limits, relationship play therapy becomes a warm, practical, living experience. It enables children to create positive emotional lives, to carry out ideas and interests freely and fully, to be alone, creative, and unafraid in the presence of an adult who shares the play process and confirms the child's individuality and autonomy.

4

Play Therapy with Self-Directed Children

*P*lay therapy offers a special opportunity for children to direct their own play activities. It offers a child–adult relationship in a setting where the boundaries are greatly expanded. In the playroom, self-directed children can express their feelings openly—their fears and anger, their resentment and disgust. They can also express their joyous and comic ways. They can act like babies at one moment and speak a garbled language and in the next moment act their own age without fear of being examined or criticized. In fantasy, self-actualizing children can be grown men and women who tell others what to do. In play therapy, self-regulated children assume many different family roles in their freely created imaginative dramas.

They need not submit to the everyday pressures of living. They can explore their feelings in any way they wish. In relationship therapy, the therapist does not set up external standards or social expectations. The therapist honors children's needs, desires, thoughts, and feelings, as expressed.

Self-Directed Children's Use of Play Therapy

Children use play therapy in varied and unique ways. In relationship therapy certain characteristics are commonly expressed by self-directed children. At various times they discuss their world directly as it exists for them. They assess the play setting, freely choose the play materials, and bring their own unique and original styles into the therapeutic relationship.

When children are attuned to their feelings, they say what bothers them. They do not hesitate to express aggressive or regressive feelings. They are not timid or subtle. They are not violent, cunning, or sadistic. At times, they may use baby talk but this behavior has a short life and they move on to more rewarding play for their development.

Children who do not have severe emotional problems almost immediately accept the therapist as a special kind of person. They employ various strategies to discover their responsibilities and the limits of play therapy. They are personally involved and happy in their play, often singing and humming. They are decisive and spontaneous. Self-regulated children express their emotions in localized and focused ways. They often recount their play therapy experiences with teachers and parents.

Perhaps the most important aspect of the play therapy experience for the self-directed child is the concentrated relationship with the therapist, created in a short span of time. In this relationship, the child is able to express frustrations or resentments, bringing them out directly in play. In this way, play therapy is a preventive mental-health experience in which children can express and explore feelings not easy to reveal at school or home.

The following case histories illustate how children who are coping with temporary family crises use the play therapy experience.

Johnny

Johnny, 4 years old, eagerly entered the playroom. During the first ten minutes, he talked about family experiences and activities of the past few weeks. He explored and tested the kind of relationship this was going to be. Seemingly satisfied that he could trust the therapist, he moved on to play. He went directly to the dollhouse and put furniture into the various rooms. He whistled and sang throughout the session. During his imaginative play, he told amusing stories about unusual incidents.

Johnny expressed himself clearly. Ordinarily, his vocabulary was extensive, yet in the playroom he used baby talk and peculiar-sounding syllables. This regressive behavior was recognized and accepted by the therapist. Johnny felt free to be himself, to play in accordance with his own interests and fantasies.

The following excerpt describes the pattern of Johnny's regressive and mature play.

First Play Session with Johnny

CHILD: (*Walks to the nursing bottles. Picks up a bottle and puts it into his mouth. Sucks on nipple for a few seconds, then replaces bottle.*) I want to take another little drink of that.

THERAPIST: You want to have another little drink, hm?

C: Yeah. (*Picks up the bottle and drinks again.*) I'm gonna take one more sip. I'm gonna take a big sip this time—a great big one. (*Takes a long drink from the bottle. Replaces bottle on the bench and walks to the dollhouse. Picks up a boy doll figure and a small rubber cat. Shouts in a baby voice.*) Whoo, whoo, whoo. Meow, meow, meow, meow. (*Holds figures over the roof of dollhouse.*) Kitty gonna jump. Baby gonna jump. Kitty jump down. Baby jump down. See-shee, see-shee, see-shee, see-shee. (*A few minutes later picks up a woman doll.*) She's a Girl Scout, and here she is. She runs with a whip. She runs with a whip.

T: Running, running, running.

C: Running. Yes, and she's ice skating, ice skating. She ice skates wherever she goes. Skating all around. (*Picks up a rubber knife.*) And there's her carving knife. She carves, she carves with her carving knife. And she carves and carves and carves. It's in the spring, so she goes around with no things on. She skates everywhere with nothing on. (*Handles doll and twists and turns it into many different positions.*) See? See? She's still ice skating. She's gonna ice skate the whole morning. She skates everywhere she goes. There she goes on the ice. Twisting and turning.

T: Twisting and turning.

C: She fishes through the ice. See? She kneels down, and she ice skates, and when she wants to catch the fish, she does. And then when she catches the fish, she's happy. Then, see? She dances.

T: Mm-hm. She dances and dances. She's so happy.

Discussion

In this session, initially Johnny's play reflects his behavioral regression. He drinks from a nursing bottle, not with the impelling urgency of a baby, yet not with hesitancy and uncertainty. His speech is, at times, immature. His voice is on a higher than usual pitch. He easily switches to mature play expressions; humming and singing, obviously very happy. His imaginative play is accepted and valued by the therapist.

Johnny's freedom-to-be registers in his choices, in his activities, and in his fantasies. The play therapist consistently affirms the values of trust, acceptance, and respect. Johnny's joy in his play expressions and in his accomplishments is obvious. He gradually shifts from caution to spontaneous dramatic play and fills the playroom with glorious laughter and sparkling energy. Play therapist and child connect in ways that inspire self-esteem and creative activity. Johnny leaves the session with exuberance and confidence as he moves toward the next moments of living authentically.

Michael

Michael, 4 years old, is described by his nursery school teacher as a "youngster who is most frequently seen with other children. He is an enthusiastic leader of his age group. He has a steady interest in structured, organized groups and activities. He is usually independent of adults in these situations. He becomes irritated when interfered with while he is engaged in games and other activities. He is alone only when he is absorbed in looking at books or listening to records. Most of his play involves imaginative construction of community and family scenes. His relations with adults are good. On his own initiative, he shares many of his special interests with teachers and with his parents."

Two individual sessions and one group session were conducted with Michael. During the first session, he described recent family experiences. He expressed some aggression, kicking and hitting the comeback toy. He explored his father's attitude of rigidly sticking to certain limits and his own feelings about that. He also showed a warm, positive identification with his father. During the second session, Michael used the nursing bottle and sucked water from it. He later took responsibility for his behavior by informing the therapist that he could tell anyone that he (Michael) had been drinking from the bottle. He also expressed his sorrow as he described the death of a neighbor.

After the second session, Michael exclaimed that he did not want to come to the playroom any more, but a month later he returned with a group. In the group session, Michael spilled water around the room and led two other children in various activities. They often looked to him for direction during the session. They did whatever he asked them to do. Sometimes he suggested to the other children that they break certain play things. At one point, he destroyed two balloons. He spent the final ten minutes of the group session painting and drawing. The other children joined him in this activity.

Excerpts from tape recordings of the two individual sessions follow.

First Play Session with Michael

    T: You can use these in any way you like, Michael.
    C: O.K. (*Points to a small gun on the table.*) My brother used to have a gun just like this one.

T: He had a gun just like that, hm?

C: Yes. Except that it wasn't filled up with clay like that one.

T: Mm-hm.

C: (*For the next seven minutes C plays quietly, shooting the gun and pushing cars and trucks around the table. Toward the end of this time he walks to the doll furniture.*) I used to have little things like these.

T: You did, hm?

C: (*Plays silently with the doll furniture, arranging the furniture in the rooms of the dollhouse. Ten minutes later he takes all the furniture out of the house and looks at the therapist.*) I have to go-go.

T: You have to go, hm? All right.

C: (*Comes back from bathroom and pats comeback toy on head. Holds shirt in hand and then puts it on.*) I don't know why Mommy wants me to wear a sweater in the house. Like here, or some place like that where it's warm. She always says, "Put it on, put it on." I don't know why she wants me to, but she just does.

T: It's hard to understand.

C: (*Points to the comeback toy.*) Is this a big balloon? What's in it that makes it so heavy? Is there just air in it?

T: It's just filled up.

C: With air. (*Hits at comeback toy.*) I really knocked it.

T: You really did knock it.

C: (*Pushes comeback toy down on the floor and sits on it.*) It's a chair now, and I'm sitting on it. Look. I'm riding on a balloon. (*Slides off comeback, grabs it and hugs it. Then kicks it around the room. Finally leaves it and picks up a small green balloon.*) You know, you can get lots more balloons, and I know where. At the dime store.

T: You could buy all you want there.

C: Yeah. 'Cause they keep bringing them and bringing more. These people do. They go pop, and you can get more.

T: Sometimes people break them, but you can always get more.

C: Yes. You know, once mine broke, and my daddy could have gotten me some more, but he wouldn't. He didn't want to.

T: Yours broke once, and your daddy didn't want to get you any more.

C: He could have. He could have if he had wanted to, but he just didn't want to.

T: Just wouldn't get you any more, though you would have liked him to.

C: Yes. (*Pause. Points to the masks.*) What are those for?

T: You can do whatever you want with them.

C: They're rubber, huh? I'm gonna put them on once and scare you.

T: You feel like scaring me.

C: Yes. I'm gonna put them all on and scare you. (*Puts each of the masks on.*)

T: Now you've scared me with all of them.

C: Yes. I've scared you with the monkey and the clown and the pig. Do you have any more here?

T: No, that's all we have.

C: Well, you know you could get some more.

T: Could we buy more?

C: *I* think you could.

T: You believe we could, hm?

C: Yes. (*Pause.*)

T: You have only a short while longer to play, Mike, and then you'll have to stop for today.

C: Why?

T: Because your time is almost up over here.

C: O.K. You know? The monkey looks the funniest of them all. Do you want to put it on?

T: Do you suppose I do?

C: Yes. (*Puts the monkey mask on the therapist and laughs. Points to the policeman figure.*) What's he doing?

T: You tell me.

C: Oh, he's just policing. How are they made?

T: What would you say about that?

C: With lead. (*Walks to the comeback toy.*) I'm gonna give him a good big kick and try to knock him down. See? There he goes.

T: You kicked him down that time.

C: Mm-hm. Twice.

T: Well, I see your time is up for now.

C: O.K. (*Leaves room with therapist.*)

Discussion

In this session, Michael expresses his negative feelings. He resents his mother's rule that he must wear a sweater in the house. He also expresses mild annoyance toward his father, who refused to buy Michael a new balloon after he had broken one. Later, he seeks the therapist's support in his feeling that when balloons are broken they can be easily replaced. For Michael, expression of feelings and the need to be heard and accepted are important in his relationships. He wants the freedom to be more aggressive and assertive without being punished.

Second Play Session with Michael

C: (*Walks into the room and points to pail of water.*) What's this for?

T: You can use it for anything you want.

C: (*During the next fifteen minutes Michael plays quietly with the airplanes and the soldiers. Then goes to the dollhouse, puts all the furniture in, and places all the doll figures on beds. Opens roof of the dollhouse, then walks to a large balloon and picks it up.*) This one is just about ready to go up. If I let go like this, if there was only a little water in it, then it would really go up. Like a blimp. And if I had air to blow it, then it could be a jet. It could be a jet

T: It could be a jet, couldn't it?

C: (*Pause.*) Did you go to camp last Sunday?

T: No, I didn't.

C: Well, you should have seen my dad's plane fly. It went clear up in the sky. It might have crashed if a real plane had gone by.

T: You were afraid that it might have crashed, huh?

C: Well, it might have. I don't know if it would have, but it didn't. (*Continues to toss balloon in the air.*) There now. It's ready. I'll see if it will fly.

T: You're trying to fly it.

C: Yes. But it's too heavy. It won't stay. (*Pause.*) This is a real nice place here.

T: You like it over here, hm?

C: Mm-hm. That balloon is going to pop.

T: It will pop?

C: No. I'm just teasing you. But maybe it would happen. Who knows?

T: It might.

C: (*Empties water from small nursing bottle into pail by squeezing nipple.*) I can fill it up with more water.

T: You could do that if you wanted to.

C: (*Takes large nursing bottle and ejects water into pail by squeezing nipple.*) This is music. It sounds like music. Yup. Just like music. (*Puts bottle in mouth and drinks from it. Squeezes more water into pail, then drinks from bottle again. Points to the nursing bottle.*) Look. Look how far down it's gone. Maybe I'll put a little more in and fill it up.

T: Maybe you will and maybe you won't.

C: Who knows? Do you want to drink from it?

T: No.

C: Then I'll give him [*comeback toy*] a drink. If he had a big hole, I'd really put water in him, and he'd get much heavier. And maybe if I got him wet, he would go pop.

T: Just go pop, that's what.

C: You know? You could give this stuff to a cow.

T: You could do that.

C: (*Sits down on the floor and moves one hand up and down in pail of water while using the other hand to hold the bottle in his mouth.*

Points to the bottle.) You know, to get this room filled with this, it takes millions and trillions of days.

T: A long time, hm?

C: A very long time.

T: A long, long time.

C: It would take near to the end of counting, and I would get so tired.

T: You'd be worn out.

C: It would take so long that I couldn't stay alive that long.

T: You couldn't live that long, hm?

C: No. On the fifteenth day I'd be a father, and on the fiftieth day I'd be an old man.

T: Just an old man, that's what.

C: Like my neighbor. You know, he died last week. He died. The last day on the calendar he died. Just last week he died.

T: Just like that he died.

C: (*Long silence.*)

T: You have only a short while longer to play, Michael.

C: I bet people will ask you who drank from here and poured all that into the pail.

T: Someone might ask those questions.

C: And then what would you say?

T: What would you want me to tell them?

C: Say that Michael T. did it.

T: All right. I'll say that to them.

C: Probably they've never seen me. And anyway, they wouldn't understand. Look at your wristwatch and see if it's time to go.

T: We have a few more minutes left.

C: Well, I'm ready to go now. I'm finished.

T: O.K.

Discussion

In his second session, Michael expresses positive feelings and identifies with his father. He proudly describes his dad's model airplanes.

The nursery school staff expressed surprise that Michael used the nursing bottle during his play sessions. His teacher indicated that she had not seen Michael use regressive behavior in the nursery school. She stated that there had been no noticeable change in Michael's behavior after his play sessions. Michael described for his teacher and his mother, in detail, what had happened in the playroom, and his enjoyment of the experience.

My impression of Michael was that he had a self-image that was important to him to maintain, at school and at home. He did not want his teachers or his parents to see his enjoyment in discovering what it was like to drink from a nursing bottle again. In the playroom he was free to experiment and to be a mature, bright 4-year-old at times and also an infant who could joyously regress in his behavior. The therapist accepted his contrasting patterns of self expression and encouraged and supported his decisions.

Joey

Joey, 3½ years old, was described by his nursery school teacher as a happy, carefree child who played well with other children and who also engaged in self-initiated activities with confidence. Only rarely did he lose control or have difficulty accepting limits in school. His intelligence-test scores fell in the superior range and he was advanced for his age in vocabulary achievement. He had an 8-year-old brother and a 2-year-old sister.

Joey visited me in the playroom three times; the sessions were one week apart. Almost from the beginning he was an uninhibited child who made decisions easily and directed his own play. The therapist's goal was to establish a relationship with Joey, affirm him as a person, and encourage his freedom and creativity in play.

At the beginning of his first session, Joey, at times, was indecisive; he asked what he should do. After twenty minutes, he said, "I didn't know what I was going to do when I came in, did I?" He made numerous decisions after the initial hesitancy. He used the comeback toy, punching and rolling on the floor with it. He expressed his affection by hugging the huge balloon figure and holding it close to him. Toward the end of the first session, Joey struggled with the problem of whether he should get paint on his hands. After a period of indecisiveness and trying other ways, he decided to paint with his hands: "I'll put all my fingers in there to get some out."

First Play Session with Joey

T: You can use these play materials in any way that you want, Joey.

C: Guns. And look! That's clay.

T: Mm-hm.

C: (*Picks up a cat balloon.*) Hey! See?

T: Mm-hm.

C: What's this? Is this a kitty cat?

T: Do you suppose that's what it is?

C: It looks like a kitty cat. (*Squeezes balloon and drops it to floor. Picks up three other balloons.*) What are these for?

T: You can use them in any way that you want.

C: (*Looks at balloons for a few seconds, then drops them on the floor. Picks one up again.*) How did this one get so dirty?

T: How would you explain it, Joey?

C: (*Sighs heavily and shrugs shoulders. Picks up a toy knife and sucks on the handle for a few seconds, then bites on the knife blade. Moves to dollhouse and picks up a male doll figure.*) What's this?

T: What would you say?

C: (*Undresses a number of boy and girl doll figures.*) This is a girl and these are her shoes. And this is something else. It's a boy. (*Takes out men and women figures and starts to undress them.*) That. That. Take off his coat. Take off his jacket. Take his hand up like that and pull it like that. And here is the baby.

T: That's the baby, hm?

C: The baby, the baby. You take it off like this and like this. And here's another baby. And this is the mommy, and this is the little boy. And this one's the girl. She's the mommy. (*Pause.*) Let's go to toidy.

T: You have to go?

C: Uh-huh.

T: All right.

C: (*Goes to the bathroom with therapist. Returns and picks up a balloon.*) You know, there should be a string here at the tail end. There should be a string to tie around all of these. (*Walks to table and picks up ball of clay. Inserts some clay in vise.*) Do you have any sticks here? Look. I'm turning this around and around in here. See? And I'm turning it over here and down here and back to here.

T: Mm-hm. You're making it go all over.

C: (*Pulls a small piece off ball of clay and grunts. Then starts pushing on the clay.*)

T: You're pushing it as hard as you can.

C: Yes. (*Grunts again.*) There. I'm gonna take a piece off. I'm gonna break a piece off. Little pieces off. See? I broke a piece. It's large enough.

T: It is, hm?

C: Yes. It's large enough. I just breaked it off.

T: You just pulled it right off.

C: I need some new pieces. And then you can roll it right up like this.

T: You just roll it and roll it and roll it.

C: It's hard. (*Holds a piece of clay. Picks up a large gun and shoots at clay.*)

T: Bang.

C: (*Puts gun down and walks over to comeback toy and hits it.*)

T: Socko.

C: Woooo. (*Pushes comeback toy down and sits on it. Bounces up and down on comeback's head and begins to breathe more heavily. Gets off comeback toy and watches it rise.*) It got up. Up. You know, I didn't know what I was going to do when I came in, did I?

T: You didn't know then, but now you know what you want to do.

C: I didn't know what I was going to play—play down here.

T: You didn't, hm?

C: (*Picks up gun and shoots comeback toy in the head.*) I shot the clown.

T: You shot the clown.

C: (*Shoots comeback again.*)

T: Bang.

C: I shot it right in his mouth. He can't talk now.

T: Right in the mouth so he'll never say anything.

C: No.

T: He'll just keep quiet.

C: Yeah. (*Goes back to the clay. Pulls a piece off and grunts.*) I took a piece.

T: Mm-hm.

C: (*Starts rolling long pieces of clay.*) You take this, and you do this.

T: Mm-hm.

C: That's the way you do it. That way and that. See?

T: Mm-hm.

C: (*Picks up gun again and shoots at clay.*)

T: Bang.

C: (*Goes to finger paints and opens jar of yellow paint. Starts to pour some of it on the paper.*) There's not little paintbrushes here, is there?

T: No, we don't have any little brushes in here, Joey.

C: (*Looks at paint on paper.*) How am I going to do that?

T: That's hard to figure out, isn't it?

C: (*Picks up scissors and moves them up and down in the yellow paint.*) Take it like this.

T: Mm-hm.

C: And then a little bit like this. (*Opens jar of blue paint and uses scissors to put some of the paint on the paper.*) Look.

T: Mm-hm.

C: It's deep. Now I'll stir it up a little. See? I didn't get paint on me, so I can use the scissors.

T: You don't want to get any paint on you, hm?

C: Uh-huh. I don't want to get it on my sweater, so I'll just have to use this. (*Rubs scissors back and forth on paint-smeared paper.*) There. Lookit.

T: You've got it all on now, hm?

C: You do this way. I have to do it.

T: Mm-hm. That's the way you have to do it.

C: I can't do it with my two hands.

T: You can't?

C: Yes. I can. (*Smears paint over paper with hands and starts to make figures.*) I can go to the bathroom, can't I?

T: If you want to. It's up to you.

C: Mm-hm. When I'm through. More paint with the scissors. More paint now. You know, the paint's pretty near gone. (*Uses the scissors to take more paint out of jars and smears it on the paper.*) Look. There's only two scissorsful left.

T: Only that much, hm?

C: You know what I should do? I should go and get some water and make some more paint.

T: That's what you want to do. Make more paint.

C: Mm-hm.

T: You have only a short while longer to play, Joey, and then we have to go back.

C: (*Pounds the clay on paper and cuts clay with scissors.*) You do it like this and then like that.

T: You pound it, hm?

C: And you cut it like this and then this. Like this.

T: Mm-hm.

C: That way. (*Sticks fingers into jar of blue paint and starts painting pieces of clay.*) This way. And this way and this and this. Just like this. I can get it out with my hand and my fingers. You take it out just like this.

T: You can take it out that way.

C: I'll get it out. My big hand's in the way. I'll put all my fingers in there to get some out. (*Finishes painting clay and then smears paint over the paper.*) Gotta paint 'em. Where should we put this to hang?

T: You mean you want to hang it up to dry?

C: I know where we can put it. We can put it right over here. Hang it
    up so it can be dry and pretty.
T: It can be dry and pretty then, hm?
C: You know, you should get pink paint at the store.
T: Pink paint?
C: Yes. So I can make a pink painting.
T: You'd like to do a pink painting, hm?
C: Yes.
T: Well, Joey, your time is up now.
C: Some day when I come again, I'm going to look and look until I
    find the pink paint.

Discussion

Joey's regression is prominent in this session, expressed in his sucking, biting, and grunting behavior. He also is aggressive, shooting frequently at the clay material and later at the comeback toy. He is careful
to shoot the clown in the mouth so that "he can't talk now," thereby
emphasizing that he does not want his behavior reported.

In the following session, Joey continues with his regressive behavior, speaking baby talk and gibberish, sucking and chewing the nipple
and drinking from a nursing bottle. The therapist accepts this behavior and encourages Joey to feel free to continue with it. Joey is concerned
about the clay, which he had gotten all over his hands. At one point, he
wants to smear the therapist with clay but accepts the therapist's limit.
He buries a dog in clay. Feeling satisfied after burying the dog and
pounding the clay, he cuts into the buried dog with scissors. Later, he
pulls the dog from the clay and moves the dog around the room, hap-
pily making loud barking sounds.

Joey rejoices in his freedom to express a range of feelings ordinarily
not acceptable. He moves with caliber and definiteness as he tests the
child–adult relationship in play therapy.

Second Play Session with Joey

C: (*Enters and goes immediately to the vise. Touches it and walks away. Pulls out a number of items from his pocket.*) I brought these over.

T: Oh, I see. You brought over a few things of your own this time.

C: Mm-hm. I brought them over 'cause I wanted to.

T: You not only wanted to bring them, but you did.

C: Mm-hm. I'm not gonna play with none of these things. I'm just gonna put them in my pocket with the rest. O.K.?

T: You're going to put them all in there.

C: (*Picks up a large gun and shoots at dollhouse.*)

T: Bang.

C: (*Walks to dollhouse and shoots through one of the windows.*)

T: Bang.

C: Oh, lookit. Here's a doggy. A doggy. (*Shoots the gun at the dog figure.*)

T: Bang. You shot the doggy.

C: I did that, but I didn't do it really, did I?

T: Just pretending, hm?

C: Mm-hm. I've got a gun at home. Not like that, though. Another kind. I have a gun, and it twists, and then it comes down like this.

T: Oh, I see. It goes way back.

C: Yes. And I have a holster, too.

T: A holster to go with the gun.

C: Doggy, doggy, doggy. (*Puts the dog in the clay and then pulls it out again.*) Woooo. Mmmmmmm. Wooo. Little doggy mine.

T: It belongs just to you.

C: These are my sunglasses and my keys.

T: Mm-hm.

C: When the sun's out it's dark and I can't see out of them. I can't.

T: Mm-hm.

C: Sometimes the sun gets in my eyes, so I have to put my sunglasses on.

T: That protects your eyes, doesn't it?

C: Keeps the sun out of my eyes. Gigigigigi. (*Hits comeback toy. Puts it down on the floor and sits on it. Wrestles with it.*) Wooo-wooo-wooo. (*Gets off comeback toy and picks up small nursing bottle.*) Take the nub off. (*Sucks on nipple and pulls nipple off bottle with teeth. Then pours water on the roof of the dollhouse.*) Oooh-oooh.

T: You like doing that, hm?

C: Yes. It's gonna get empty. Wooo-wooo. (*Refills bottle with water and hands nipple to therapist.*) Put it on. (*Replaces small nursing bottle on bench and drinks from large bottle.*) Weee-weee. Mmmm-mmm-mmmm.

T: You like to drink from that bottle.

C: Hmm?

T: You like to drink from that bottle.

C: (*Picks up gun and shoots at therapist.*) Na-na-na-na-na. (*Throws gun into pail of water.*) Mmmm-mmm-mmmm. (*Continues to drink from bottle.*) Aaah-aah. (*Puts down large nursing bottle and picks up small one. Pours water from it on roof of dollhouse.*) It's getting all over the floor. It got on me. I'm gonna go in the bathroom and wipe my pants. (*Takes scissors and cuts clay. Puts small pieces of clay into toy sink.*) Get this soft. Get this soft.

T: It's going to be soft, hm?

C: It's going to be. Wooooo-wooooo. (*Takes dog and buries it in clay.*) Doggy, doggy, doggy gone.

T: Gone away, hm?

C: So nobody will know.

T: You don't want anyone to know.

C: No one knows that he's there, do they?

T: You don't want anybody to know, hm?

C: (*Picks up dog, which is covered with soggy clay, and pushes it toward therapist.*)

T: You want to put it on me, but you may not do that.

C: (*Buries dog in clay again. Cuts bit pieces of clay.*) Whole big pieces. Pieces and pieces and pieces. (*Takes dog out of clay.*) Bow. Bow-wow. Bow-wow-wow. (*Pause.*) O.K. I want to go back now.

T: All right. You still have a while left, but if you'd like to leave now, it's up to you.

C: Yes. Let's go.

Discussion

Joey begins this session by shooting the gun at the house and later shooting the dog figure. His aggressive play continues in his attack on the clown.

Joey's language and behavior are immature at points. He drinks from the nursing bottle and sucks and chews on the nipple. As he expresses these feelings again and again, they become less and less intense. He achieves full satisfaction and moves on to other play activities.

Third Play Session with Joey

During the third session, Joey discards his baby talk and does not return to the nursing bottles. He focuses most of his time on the clay and paints, very freely cutting the clay and soaking it with paints. Playing through his feelings in an unrestricted fashion, Joey proudly makes a little boy. Uninhibited in speech and movement, he uses his hands while painting spontaneously, revealing his inner freedom. Whereas in an earlier session clay was repeatedly pulled apart into little pieces, in this session the clay is used creatively as Joey makes friendly dogs with fur. He acknowledges responsibility for his behavior, clearly indicating to the therapist his intentions and goals.

Following the third play session, a conference was held with the nursery school staff, at which time Joey's teacher expressed surprise that he had sucked water from the nursing bottles and used baby talk. She also stated that she had never seen him use clay as he had in play therapy. His teacher reported that after the first session Joey had exhibited occasional unrestrained outbursts and made unusual demands of others. Within a short period of time, however, these patterns disappeared.

Play therapy provided self-directed children with an opportunity to meet with an adult in a therapeutic relationship, in and through which the child's concerns and fantasies could be fully expressed and explored, in self-chosen activities consistent with the child's interests and desires.

5

Situational Play Therapy

*O*ver the years of my work as a child therapist, I have found play therapy to be effective with children facing a disturbing new family experience that they perceive as threatening. I have viewed these meetings as a form of situational play therapy, typically consisting of a brief therapy—three individual play sessions and, in some instances, one group play session.

In the two cases described here in some detail, the children were faced with one of the commonest crises of childhood, the arrival of a new baby in the family. Of a number of instances in which play therapy sessions were equally effective, the two examples provide interesting, clear-cut illustrations of situational therapy.

The New-Baby Crisis

Self-directed children who experience such catastrophes as a fire or flood, or who have had to cope with accidents or illnesses, or who are subjected to such family crises as divorce and death often show confusion, distress, aggression, and anxiety. The arrival of a new baby in the family is a common, temporary disturbance of childhood. Such an event brings a period of stress, for however stable, well-organized, and loving family relationships may be, the arrival of a new family member requires some changes in behavior and in the ways of relating to each person in the family. Family disorganization may result, at least temporarily, and the older child or children may be faced with a difficult period of adjustment.

For neither Tommy nor Susan, whose play therapy sessions are reported, was the arrival of a new baby a surprise. Both had been informed of the coming event several months in advance, and both had expressed pleasure in the prospect.

Tommy

Tommy, 4 years old, had been regarded as a happy child, both personally and socially, by his nursery school teacher, the nursery school director, and the school psychologist. His relations with other nursery school children were positive. He spoke with pride of his home and parents. His parents viewed Tommy as a secure, confident child who easily accepted limits and responsibilities.

When Tommy was 4½ years old, an adopted girl of 13 was suddenly brought into the home, and three months later his mother gave birth to a daughter. During this period, Tommy's behavior showed a radical change, both at school and at home. At school, he became sulky, refused to accept even simple, clear, and reasonable limits, retreated from child groups whenever things did not go his way, and often withdrew into long sessions of solitary play. At home, he became fidgety. At mealtimes, he refused to eat foods that he had previously enjoyed. He cried often. On one occasion, he attempted to destroy the family record player. He was often ill tempered and irritable. His mother, after attempting to deal with the situation by explanations and supports of many kinds, contacted the psychologist and requested play therapy for Tommy.

Three play sessions were held with Tommy. During the first, he played with airplanes and trucks the entire time and was relatively quiet. In the second session, Tommy focused on himself and the two new members of the family. He initially perceived them as potential threats, but once he had recognized these feelings and they had been accepted and clarified, he could include his siblings and share himself with them. Excerpts from the second tape-recorded session follow.

Second Play Session with Tommy

T: You can use these things in the playroom in any way that you want, Tommy.

C: You know what? I could make a little castle out of that. (*Indicates sand in sandbox.*)

T: You could make a castle.

C: These are two boats. Look.

T: Mm-hm.

C: You know what kind? This one is a ship, and this one is a ferry. This is the ocean. (*Points to sand.*) This is the way that they use them in New Mexico. Now do you know what we have to do? We have to get some water and smooth it. (*Refers to sand.*) You know what I can do? I can make an ocean liner and put it in the sand.

T: You can do that.

C: Then this can be the dock. (*Points to hill of sand.*) Then the ocean liner can go on it. It can go right on the hill.

T: Mm-hm.

C: There is just room for two boats to be on it. There. Now I'll make another boat. This can be the parking space. (*Points to spot in the sand.*) See? This is a great big parking lot for it.

T: A great big one.

C: See? This is where the little boat goes. He goes way up there. There's a parking lot for the big boat and one for the little boat. We have to do this over at the dock. Toot, toot, toot go the boats.

Look where this boat has to go. He goes to get the sand. I'm putting it right in.

T: You're putting it right inside.

C: I'm pretending this is a ship. This is where they really go. Right over here. (*Points to spot in sand.*)

T: That's really the place for them to go.

C: This [*sand*] is the stuff that they carry into the dock. Look what he has to do. He's going to bury this whole big boat.

T: He'll bury the whole big boat.

C: See? I can bury him. So no one will ever find him again.

T: He will be lost for good.

C: He'll be lost for good. It can't get out now. You see, this is the little boat's dock, and no one ever goes in this dock. Because that's his dock. You see, these two boats are brother boats.

T: One is the brother of the other one.

C: Yeah. One is the brother of the other one. Hey! Who messed my dock up? "Well, I did," says the big boat. See? He has some sand in him. He carries people in his boat, and this one has sand in his, too.

T: They both have sand.

C: You know what? They dump out the sand there. He [*little boat*] scrubs his boat off. Both of them go. You know where they're going now? In the—in the brink the ship goes first [*big boat*]. Say, what do you know, Joe? I have to make another dock for this boat [*little boat*].

T: What do you know?

C: This is the little boat. I have to build so many docks around here.

T: So many docks you have to build.

C: Yes, and all these are brothers. This is the best one (*picks up middle boat*), because, look. He can carry more sand than the other ones.

T: He's the best one of all. They're all brothers.

C: Yes. And they all have some docks, but he [*middle boat*] has the coziest one.

T: He has the nicest, coziest one.

C: And this [*big boat*] and this [*little boat*] each have one, but he [*middle boat*] can carry nice soft dirt for people to the lake. (*Picks up policeman figure and gestures toward boats.*) And this one. You know what? I'm pretending that this is an oil place, and that's where the boats get their power. You know, they don't have any power when they start off. They come around, and after a while they put their boats in this place where they can get power.

T: That's what they do.

C: I know what I'm doing. You know what I'm pretending? This is all the family, the whole family, the whole family. This is the family.

T: You're pretending it's the whole family.

C: Yeah. I have to. Well, what do you know? What do you know, Joe? What do you know, Joe? Linga, linga, linga, linga, linga, linga. Hey! I'm pretending. You see these cowboys? They're the guards.

T: They are the guards, huh?

C: All of them. They're the guards of these garages.

T: They guard them.

C: They guard them. There's the guard. You see, if anyone comes around to steal the boats—well, they'll shoot them.

T: They shoot anyone who tries to steal the boats.

C: This is the best cowboy, and he guards this boat (*middle boat*). Linga, linga, linga. You know what? They watch to see that no one steals anything. They watch the garages, too. One guard in front of each garage. This guard watches this [*big boat*]. This guard watches this [*middle boat*]. And this guards this one [*little boat*]. This guy [*middle boat*] is lucky. He's lucky because he has the nicest house, the nicest house of all. He has the best house of all. He can just fit in right well. These [*the other two boats*] are lucky, too. They have power. They squeeze right in. He has power, too. He goes over and gets his power.

T: You have just a short while longer to play.

C: Hey, ring, ring! It's me. I'm your brother. It's all right. I was here before you, but come with me. Hey! Big boat and little boat say, "Please give me some power," and middle boat says, "O.K."

Middle boat: "I'm going to get more power. Hey, Joe. Come on. I'll help you. We've got the best house in the world. We'll get some power. All we'll have to do is back right out and get it. We can get our power and gas easy." Linga, linga, linga. We can go now. When others come in, they'll be able to see that I built all this.

Discussion

In relationship play therapy, Tommy approaches the difficulties of suddenly being confronted with two new family members. He feels that his status in the family is precarious. In his play, he first builds a dock and an ocean for the ships. Next, he makes a parking lot with spaces for two boats. He uses a policeman to protect his possessions, and makes sure that his own boat is the nicest boat, the coziest boat, the best boat of all. The parking lot becomes a garage that is transformed into a home. In the end, the boats become "brother boats," and Tommy shares his "power" with his siblings. He exclaims, "We've got the best house in the world."

The therapeutic process for Tommy included opportunities to express, again and again, negative feelings toward his new siblings, ambivalent feelings, in which he shifted back and forth between anger and joy, and positive feelings in which he shared his belongings, including his home, with his siblings.

After the third play session, which was similar to the second, Tommy decided not to return to the playroom. His mother reported that he had informed her directly, "Look here, Mother. There are some things that are mine. They belong to me, and there are other things that I can share and will gladly share." His mother responded, "Of course, Tommy. That's the way it will always be."

The nursery school staff and Tommy's parents reported that Tommy once again had become the affable, free, expressive child they had known before the arrival of his siblings.

Susan

The nursery school staff described Susan, 3 years old, as a charming youngster whose winning smile and understanding ways had made her popular with both children and adults. Her mother considered Susan's relations with an older sibling excellent. When Susan was 3 years and 3 months old, a new baby arrived in the family. Two days after the mother and the new baby daughter arrived home, Susan became babyish, immature, and whining. This behavior was evident in the nursery school as well. Susan's mother frantically telephoned the nursery school one day to ask whether something could be done to stop Susan's constant whining, which was annoying everyone in the family.

The nursery school staff referred Susan to the play therapist, who conducted three play sessions with her. During the first two sessions, Susan expressed negative feelings toward the new baby. Once her feelings were recognized and accepted, they no longer dominated her world. In her last play session, she picked up the balloon baby figure, kissed it, tossed it into the air, and danced around the room while she held it in her arms.

Excerpts from the recordings of the three sessions follow.

First Play Session with Susan

> (*Mother and child walk into the room together.*)
> THERAPIST: You can use these in any way you like.
> (*Mother starts to leave room, and child looks at her.*)
> CHILD: No, you stay here for a while.
> MOTHER: Watch the watch. When this hand gets over here, I'll be back.
> C: O.K. I'll bounce two balls.
> T: Two at a time.
> M: I'll lay down the watch where you can watch it.
> C: O.K. It's not ticking.
> M: Want me to put it on you? (*Places watch on C's wrist.*) Bye. You can just keep your eye on that watch.

C: (*Waves good-bye to mother.*) Where's the baby?

T: Where do you suppose the baby could be?

C: Here? That's the baby. Lookit the big baby. This is a balloon head. Mr. Balloon Head. (*Picks up a balloon in the form of a human figure. Squeezes balloon and cries, "Mommy, mommy, mommy."*)

T: That's what the baby cries. Mommy, mommy, mommy.

C: (*Continues to squeeze balloon and cry "Mommy, mommy, mommy." Looks at T and places balloon on table. Turns handle of vise.*) What is it?

T: You want to know what it could be.

C: A can opener. Now I'm gonna be a clown. This goes oink, oink, oink, too. Oink, oink.

T: The clown goes oink, oink.

C: Oink, oink, oink. (*Laughs.*) Now I'm gonna be a baby and drink from the bottle of water. Shall I?

T: That's up to you.

C: Should I sprinkle here? Here. Open your hand.

T: You want to sprinkle my hand.

C: (*Sprinkles water in T's hand.*) Rub them together. (*Drinks from bottle and then replaces it on bench. Turns handle of vise again.*) Now I have to can-opener this. (*Puts figure balloon into vise; it squeaks.*) She doesn't want to be can-openered.

T: She doesn't?

C: No. I heard my mummy walking. Hey! It's almost up to here. This number right there. (*Indicates number on wrist watch.*) I hear her coming.

T: You hear her coming.

C: (*Turns handle of vise. Shakes it back and forth. Looks at nursing bottles. Again turns vise handle and looks out window. Picks up figure balloon and squeezes it; drops it and steps on it.*) I'm gonna throw the ball. You kick it like that.

T: Mm-hm. That's what you do to it.

C: See what you do? Rocky-rocky the baby to sleep. Where's the baby? Where is she? Here's a mirror.

T: Mm-hm.

C: (*Peers in mirror of dresser.*) Tick-tick.

T: That's the way it goes.

C: Tick-tock. Tick-tock. There's the baby in there. (*Points to doll-house.*) Baby walking upstairs. One, two, three, four, five. Into your beds. They're in their beds. Into your bed you go, bad girl. [*Baby doll.*] And this one is a big girl.

T: A big girl.

C: With a round head. Walk, walk, walk. Here's the daddy going to bed now. Walky, walky, walky. Right next to the girl. [*Middle doll.*]

T: Mm-hm.

C: And here's the mommy. Walky, walky, walky. Right next to the baby. (*Undresses male doll.*) I'm taking his pantsies off.

T: Mm-hm. You're taking his pants off.

C: Walk, walk, walk. Walking up to bed, walking up to bed. Three little children.

T: Three little children and two big people.

C: And another little baby. Here's me. I'm taking her clothes off. I'm going to bed. Now he's up. [*Male doll.*] Up and up and up. (*Dressing male doll.*) Little up, little up. Put your pants back on. Walky, walky, walky downstairs. [*Female doll.*] Walky, walky, walky downstairs. [*Male doll.*] Walky, walky, walky. [*Another male doll.*] (*Walks baby doll downstairs.*) I'm climbing up this ladder. Let's climb up the ladders. Just climbing up the ladders.

T: Mm-hm.

C: And the little one on top of the bed. [*Middle doll.*] The little one sleeps under the bed. [*Baby doll.*]

T: One on top, one underneath.

C: Two underneath. Here's the bedroom. (*Bends figure balloon and squeezes it.*) I like that noise. Squeak, squeak, squeak. This is a big bed. Here's your bed.

T: That's my bed, huh?

C: Who sleeps in *that bed*?

T: Anyone you want.

C: Me. (*Points to watch on arm.*) That's my mother's watch. Just pretend it's your supper. (*Turns handle of vise.*) Zoom, zoom, zoom,

zoom. Here's your supper. Eat it up. Don't eat my mother's watch up. Just eat your supper up. Zoom, zoom, zoom. Here's your watch. Zoom, zoom, zoom. Here's your watch.

Discussion

In this session, Susan immediately asks for the baby. The therapeutic process begins with Susan expressing strong feelings, squeezing the balloon and mimicking the baby, resentfully. The angry expressions continue as she attempts to crush the baby's head in a vise. Then Susan expresses a desire to "can-opener" the baby. Later, she drinks from the baby bottle, perhaps indicating a strong interest in being a baby again. She crushes the baby balloon figure in the vise, steps back, appears frightened, and imagines her mother approaching. Calm again, Susan repeatedly attacks the baby balloon figure, squeezing it, dropping it, and throwing and kicking it. Susan's angry expressions continue as she throws the baby doll under the bed. She places herself between the mother and father, asserting her right to be there.

Second Play Session with Susan

C: (*Talks to mother.*) Are you gonna stay here? Here's a balloon. (*Waves a balloon figure at* T.) Good-bye (*to mother*). Mommy, leave your watch here. I want to see what time it is. (*Looks at* T's *watch.*) It will still be there tomorrow. (*Puts balloon figure in upper part of dollhouse. Empties bag of dolls.*) There. In the garbage can. (*Walks to nursing bottles.*) I'm gonna drink from this. (*Drinks from large bottle and replaces it on bench.*) He's gonna shoot you. (*Cowboy figure.*) Bang. Shoot you and tie you up. All cowboys are shooting. (*Handles soldiers and shoots* T *a few times.*) Everyone is shot. (*Squeezes figure balloon and it squeaks. Walks figure balloon up the stairs of dollhouse.*) Walk, walk, walk. (*Throws figure balloon aside. Sits on floor, fingers stairway. Picks up figure balloon and whispers.*) She's going to sleep. Shall I take her head off?

T: That's up to you.

C: (*Places balloon in box with blocks.*) That's a block. (*Picks up figure balloon again, brushes it against T's face.*) I wanta take your glasses off.

T: You'd like to do that, but that's one thing I won't let you do.

C: Let's pretend to play school. O.K.? And you're the teacher. O.K.?

T: And I'm the teacher.

C: (*Cuts a piece of paper and folds it in half. Cuts paper along folded line and into quarters. Looks at T, folds paper again and shows it to T.*) I'm gonna give these to my mother. That's for Mother's Day.

T: A Mother's Day present?

C: Yeah. (*Cuts another piece of paper in two.*) This is my mother's present, too.

T: You have quite a few to give your mother. You like to give her presents, huh?

C: (*Holds papers in hand.*) These are my mother's and my daddy's, too. Just for my mother and daddy. (*Lifts comeback toy.*) He's a big clown.

T: Mm-hm.

C: (*Carries comeback toy to T.*) There. Walk, walk, walk, walk, walk.

T: There you go.

C: (*Leans against comeback toy, pushing it down.*)

T: You want it to go down.

C: Yeah. (*Pushes comeback toy into sandbox.*) He's crying.

T: You're making him cry.

C: Yeah. (*Finally succeeds in pushing comeback toy into sandbox.*) He's crying. Nobody's taking him out.

T: He is just going to stay in there all the time.

C: (*Hands T papers that she has cut.*) Will you fold these for my mother? And my dad.

T: For no one else.

C: Not even you.

T: Not even me.

C: No. (*Starts to cut paper again. Continues. Folds one half-sheet in two again and places it on top of the others.*) See? Some's for my family, and not for you, either.

T: Not for me.

C: No. (*Cuts more paper.*) Only one is for you, and this is all you're getting. Here. None for your mother. No. It's all mine and my mother's.

T: Just yours and your mother's.

C: I'll be the teacher and gather up your things. O.K., honey. Let's, honey. Yes, honey. Where's that paper? And you, honey. Honey, honey. I'm gonna sprinkle some. (*Drops a handful of sand from sandbox into pail of water. Watches it. Takes more sand and drops it into pail. Looks at T and laughs.*) It's all getting brown, isn't it? (*Throws more sand into pail.*) The floor is getting wet. (*Continues to drop handfuls of sand into pail.*) It's getting brown water.

T: Yes, it is. It's getting to be brown water.

C: (*Throws more sand into pail.*) I splashed my shoe. See? (*Sprinkles some sand over comeback toy. Drops more sand into pail and waves her hands in the air.*) I wanta go wash them.

T: You want to wash them? O.K.

C: (*Leaves room with T.*)

Discussion

Susan begins this session expressing anger toward her entire family, throwing the family doll figures in the garbage can. Feeling free, Susan drinks from the large nursing bottle. She shoots the therapist and ties him up. Susan returns to the object of her strongest negative feelings, her baby sister. She squeezes and squeaks the baby balloon figure and fluctuates between pulling off her head and putting her to sleep.

Another level of the therapeutic process begins. Susan expresses positive feelings for her mother and father, making them presents. She shows mixed emotions toward the therapist, telling him there will be no presents for him or his mother and then calling him "honey" a number of times. Though unclearly expressed, there appears to be a beginning of positive feelings for the baby.

At the end of the session Susan drops handfuls of sand in the water and delights in hearing the sounds and seeing the brown color. She appears to be relaxed and satisfied as the session ends.

Third Play Session with Susan

C: (*Waves good-bye to mother and runs into the room. Drops a handful of sand into pail of water.*)

T: It went right in, didn't it?

C: Look how much. (*Drops another, larger handful into pail and laughs.*) A big splash. Splash. The water's getting brown. (*Drops two more handfuls of sand into the pail.*)

T: It's getting browner and browner.

C: Mmm. Now I'm making pie. (*Plays in sandbox.*) Here's your pie.

T: Is that for me?

C: Mmm. Take a shovel and eat it. Take a spoon and eat it.

T: You want me to eat it.

C: (*Throws more sand into pail and smiles at T.*) O.K. Here. (*Gestures toward T with shovel.*)

T: You want me to eat with that, huh?

C: Not really.

T: You just want me to pretend.

C: Yes. (*Fills mold with sand, pats it, and gives it to T.*) Eat it.

T: You want me to eat it now.

C: And then I'll give you some more. Eat it up. O.K. Now eat it.

T: Suppose that I don't want any more?

C: Then you won't get any dessert. Now eat it all up. O.K., now take it. Now pick it up now. Hello, hello, hello, hello. (*Dials telephone.*) Pretend I hear the phone bell ringing, and I say "Hello," and you talk.

T: Oh, all right. We'll pretend that.

C: Hello?

T: Hello.

C: Who is this?

T: Who is that?

C: This is Susan, and she's playing here. Good-bye.

T: Good-bye. (*Sneezes.*)

C: God bless you. (*Picks up large bottle and drinks. Replaces it on bench.*) I like to play here.

T: You like coming here and playing.

C: (*Walks over to balloon figure and kisses it. Tosses it into air and catches it several times while dancing around the room.*)

T: Well, our time is up for today, Susan.

C: One more bouncy and I'll go up.

T: O.K.

C: (*Throws balloon figure into air one more time. Lets it fall on floor.*) O.K. Good-bye, good-bye. Good-bye, Mister.

T: Good-bye.

Discussion

Susan continues in her play to drop sand into water, enjoying the browner and browner coloring of the water. The feeling tones of her play are more positive. She shares her "pie" with the therapist. Later, she gives him supper and tells him that unless he eats he won't get any dessert.

Susan's feelings toward her baby sister, as expressed in play dramas, are now positive. She takes the baby balloon figure, kisses it, tosses it into the air, and dances around the room, holding the baby close.

The key aspects of the play therapy process with Susan may be summarized as follows: (1) direct expression of anger toward the baby, (2) the anger becoming hesitant and ambivalent, and (3) positive feelings and definite interest in her baby sister.

Susan's mother contacted the therapist to tell him that Susan was again a pleasant child and that she was no longer afraid to leave Susan with the baby. Susan began showing affection for her baby sister and assumed some responsibilities in the baby's care.

Benefits of Play Therapy for Tommy and Susan

Tommy and Susan used symbolic forms to focus their anxiety connected with a new baby in the family. The gains in both cases involved a growing acceptance of the new sibling and feelings of security and comfort in the home. What these children needed was an opportunity to express their negative attitudes in a therapeutic relationship, that is, one in which they felt that the therapist accepted their expressions of a range of feelings and respected their preferences and individuality.

Situational play therapy provided these children with an opportunity to work out temporarily disturbing feelings and thus removed the possibility that these feelings would lose their connection to reality, become distorted, and perhaps eventually seriously damage the child. Freed from these feelings, the children were able to use their energies more effectively in personal and social interactions with other children and adults.

6

*Play Therapy
with Disturbed Children*

Dorie, 6 years old, experiences extreme mood shifts, contrasting emotional patterns that struggle for supremacy in her everyday world. Her fluctuating moods capriciously envelop her. Sometimes she is restless and nervous, moving about rapidly and with great energy, talking loudly and incessantly. She is unable to concentrate, to study or play, in a sustained fashion. At other times she is quiet, speechless, almost motionless, laboring for long periods over a single problem or task. In her hyperactive state, she jumps quickly from one activity to another. She may be heard shouting over and over again, "What'll I do first? What'll I do first?" She can be completely oblivious to the world of children and adults around her. Often, she does not listen, she does not hear, she does not respond. Adults in her environment view her as a strange child—jerky, peculiar, and bizarre in mannerisms and behavior.

Disturbed children like Dorie attract attention. They are sometimes seen by their teachers as uncontrollable, wildly aggressive, cruel, demanding, and moody. On other occasions, they are perceived as anxious, frightened, painfully silent, remote from other children and adults. Some disturbed children spend their time alone. Others continually bicker and fight. Many of these children refuse to make decisions or assume responsibilities.

Parents often describe disturbed children as selfish, mean, stubborn, hostile, inconsiderate, difficult to handle. They complain, too, that they are not teachable, that they do not seem to want to learn from others, and that they are inconsiderate and disrespectful.

Disturbed children are trapped in a restricted or closed world. Their self-concept is that of an inferior person, unloved and inadequate. They fear punishment and yet are defiant. Reward and approval rarely have a constructive effect. However inadequate they may feel, they struggle to maintain a private inner life, regardless of external allurements. Punishment only reinforces the child's own feelings of insecurity and fear and evokes determination to remain within the safe and familiar patterns of life, or to fight for survival.

The relationship play therapist does not employ reward and approval, or punishment and criticism, or pressure children to change. In relationship therapy, the child is viewed as a person with resources for working out difficulties, and moving in positive and creative directions. Disturbed children are respected in their own ways of being, in their peculiar expressions, in their fears, silences, hatreds, and resentments. They use the therapeutic relationship to express and explore underlying feelings which in the past were too threatening to reveal. When risky feelings are accepted, disturbed children reach out and begin to trust the therapist. They express themselves without feeling ashamed or guilty. They project their feelings onto media such as paints, clay, sand, and water, using these materials symbolically, giving them personal meanings. In the process, they learn to make decisions and to act spontaneously and confidently. They experiment, explore, and discover who they are and in the process gain a realistic picture of their potentials and skills.

Some children remain essentially silent in their first few play sessions. They speak to the therapist only with great reluctance. They are cautious and hesitant. They play in a small area of the room and with only a few toys. They often want to be told what to do and what not to do.

Some children maintain a rapid-fire flow of words. They may threaten to be violent and destroy play materials. They may attack the therapist. Richard, 7 years old, a typical troubled child, screamed force-fully, violently:

> C: I'll drill the whole place full of lead! Do you hear me? I'm gonna dirty this place up so far that I don't think you'll ever be able to clean this stuff up with all the water in the world. I'm gonna re-ally fix this stuff, I'm telling you. I'm gonna mess this room up like a coyote. And then I'll take this jackknife and cut everything up. Then I'll try it on you next!
> T: You want to show me how angry you can be.
> C: By George, I am angry! And nobody will be able to clean this damn place up ever again!

Whether passive or stormy, through individual ways of shaping and directing life in play and in the relationship with the therapist, each child works through disturbances of self and in the process becomes a person in the real world.

Linda

Linda, 4 years old, an only child, was considered seriously disturbed by her nursery school teacher and by the school psychologist. In school, she either shut everyone out and remained completely by herself, sitting and staring at things, or became extremely aggressive toward others, attacking other children and interfering with their play. She had no friends in school. She was rarely constructively involved with other children. Most of her contacts with teachers were characterized by whining behavior. Her nursery school teacher described Linda as moody and unpredictable. Her mother bitterly denounced her as an obstinate, willful, destructive child at home and a frightened, retiring child away from home. Her mother agreed to the play therapy but was pessimistic that it would be of any value.

Background data available on the family included the mother's exaggerated emphasis on cleanliness, the parents' feelings that Linda would never amount to much, their frequent threatening of Linda, and their belief that she would always be a child without "spark."

Linda began play therapy as part of her scheduled play sessions, in conjunction with the nursery school program. The brief series was extended to eight sessions of individual play therapy. Then her mother abruptly and without explanation began to bring her for appointments irregularly, and finally not at all. During her experiences in the playroom, Linda changed her attitudes to some degree toward herself and others. In the beginning hours of play therapy, she was a frightened, restricted child, insecure and indecisive. She typically played in mutelike silence. After several meetings, she became very talkative, decisive, and spontaneous in her play. She also became demanding in her relationship with the therapist.

Although the therapist did not feel that Linda had fully worked through her anger toward people, he felt that she had come a long way in expressing and exploring this attitude. Excerpts from Linda's play therapy sessions follow.

First Play Session with Linda

During Linda's first session she remained completely silent. She seemed to be frightened and suspicious of the play situation and the therapist. She approached the materials cautiously, confining her play to a few toys, which she used in a small space, and to the doll furniture, which she crammed into one room of a large dollhouse. When Linda entered the playroom, she walked immediately to a small table with numerous toys. She stood almost motionless, staring at the toys for a few minutes. The therapist could detect no clear emotional expression on her face. Apathetically she picked up a small truck and looked at it for quite a while. She then lined up a few trucks and made a circle of them. She crammed an airplane, truck, and boat into a small space. On top of these toys she placed a large gun. Then she quickly stepped away from the table and just stood staring at what she had created.

During the next ten minutes, Linda arranged every object on the table in orderly rows. After this, she built three high columns of toys. Once again Linda moved away from the table and stared at the toys for quite some time. Then she glanced quickly around the room and for a few seconds focused her attention on the dollhouse and furniture. She moved lethargically toward the house. She looked at the doll figures, picked them up, and undressed them very slowly. Then she put each of them under a separate bed. Linda spent the remainder of the first session forcing every piece of doll furniture into one small room of the dollhouse.

Second Play Session with Linda

This session began where the first had ended. Linda walked slowly to the dollhouse, knelt before it, and began placing furniture in it. This time she expanded her attention to two rooms of the house. When she had difficulty fitting some pieces of furniture into the rooms, she put them on top of other pieces, until the two rooms were huge masses of furniture. Linda then undressed each of the doll figures. She pulled off the head of a large male doll, looked at the detached body for a while, and then replaced the head. She shoved all the dolls together on two beds.

Toward the end of the session Linda took some furniture from the two crowded rooms and placed it on the floor of the playroom. She dressed the male and female figures and placed them face down on the floor. Once again she was completely silent during this session.

Third Play Session with Linda

In the third play session, Linda radically shifted her behavior. She talked incessantly throughout the entire session. At first, she wanted to be told what to do. She repeatedly asked for reassurance and often asked for help. Later in the session, she made decisions on her own and carried them out. She approached her reported phobia of knives by examining the knives in the playroom. She asked about them, and used them in her play. She projected her anger onto people figures. She wanted to bathe the family dolls in red paint: "I'll put some people in there, and then they'll get all red. They'll be red all over." Linda did not carry out this threat. Instead, she expressed her anger in water play, throwing water all over the floor, stamping around in it, and screaming over and over again as she ran back and forth.

Following are excerpts from this third session.

C: (*Enters and slowly, carefully examines room. Walks to workbench and points to jars of finger paints.*) What is this?

T: What do you suppose?

C: (*Very softly.*) I don't know.

T: You just don't know what's in there.

C: Paint. (*Tries to open a jar of paint, then hands it to therapist.*) Open this.

T: It's kind of hard to do, isn't it? (*Therapist opens a jar.*)

C: What is it?

T: What does it look like to you?

C: I don't know. What do we use it for?

T: Well, you can use it in any way you want.

C: (*Opens all the jars of paint, dumps a box of crayons on workbench.*) Crayons. There's a green and white and brown and yellow.

T: All different colors, hm?

C: This is pink.

T: Mm-hm.

C: That one's brown.

T: Mm-hm.

C: They fell out.

T: Mm-hm.

C: (*Points to rubber knives.*) Can I paint those that are down there?

T: You decide for yourself.

C: (*Picks up a rubber knife.*) Well, what is this?

T: What could it be, Linda?

C: I don't know. (*Pause.*) A knife. It's a knife.

T: That's what it is, hm? A knife.

C: (*Points to knife sheath.*) Why can it come out of here for?

T: Why do you suppose?

C: I know why. It's to use it. Could I—? (*Pause.*) Could I take it home?

T: You want to take it home, Linda, but I can't let anything go out of the playroom.

C: Why?

T: Why do you suppose?

C: No child could play with it then. (*Picks up small toy table.*) Can I paint this?

T: You can do whatever you like here. It's up to you.

C: I *want* to paint it. How do you paint with this stuff?

T: That's difficult to figure out, isn't it?

C: I want to paint something. I want to paint something. I don't want to paint it with my hands.

T: You want to paint but not with your hands, hm?

C: I want to do it with something. Can you give me anything to do it with?

T: What would you suggest?

C: (*Starts cutting small pieces from edge of paper.*) What's in that door over there?

T: Oh, that's just a storage room.

C: I want to go in there and see.

T: You want to go in the room and see. Well, that room is locked. There's no way of getting into it unless you have a key.

C: Why don't you have a key? Will you help me finish this Christmas tree?

T: What would you like me to do, Linda?

C: You could draw it on there, and I'll cut it.

T: Well, you'll have to show me how to do it. Where shall I begin?

C: Well, it goes like this. All the way from here to here. (*Outlines the tree on the paper.*) Now it looks like a Christmas tree.

T: It does. Just like a Christmas tree.

C: It goes in and out, in and out on two sides. (*Cuts out the tree and places it on the table. Looks at paints.*) I don't want to put it on with my hands. Could I use a crayon?

T: That's up to you, Linda.

C: I could put some paint on here and put it on the paper. (*Dips crayon into paint jar and smears the paint on paper. Then points to Christmas tree.*) It's sticky. Now I'll paint this.

T: Mm-hm.

C: There. Now I can close it up here and paint it up to there. (*Picks up pieces of furniture and paints them. Takes a toy table and paints it red.*) Now look what kind it is.

T: What kind is it now?

C: You guess.

T: Let's see, what might it be?

C: Red. It's red. (*Smears yellow paint over red paint.*) Now it's yellow. And now it's blue. The next child to come over—. What will you have for her?

T: You tell me, Linda.

C: Just the same things. Just what's here now. Now the next time I'm gonna paint up the window.

T: That's what you'll do, hm?

C: (*Picks up toy dressing table and paints the mirror.*) It's painted red. (*Paints the bathtub with red paint.*) It's red all over. Drown them.

T: You want to drown them?

C: I'll put them in there and get them all red. They'll be red all over.

T: You'd like to see them get all red.

C: (*Points to bathtub.*) In here. In here. That's where to put them. All red. All red. And I'm gonna do it now.

T: You'll put them in right now.

C: (*Stares at the family doll figures for a few seconds.*) I'm gonna go wash my hands. I can turn the light on by myself.

T: O.K. You only have a few minutes left, Linda, and then we'll have to stop for today.

C: (*Returns from bathroom.*) How come there are two knives here?

T: For whatever you want to use them.

C: I'd like to take one home and leave the other one here.

T: Well, you can't take anything out of the playroom, Linda.

C: I'm gonna put one around me and buckle it. (*Puts both knives around her waist. Then holds one knife in each hand and pushes balloons around the room, first with one knife and then with the other, making wild motions. Suddenly runs to large nursing bottle and pours water on the floor. Empties pail of water on floor. Runs into bathroom to get another pailful of water and overturns this on the floor. Laughs very hard and stamps around in the water as the play session ends, yelling unintelligibly and screaming angrily at everything in the room.*)

Discussion

Linda launches her experiences in play therapy with silent, anxious, frightened expressions of self. Her fears are vague, unclear, without focus. She appears reluctant to use the toys and is suspicious. Her feelings remain hidden, and yet there is a deep tension in her movements. Only gradually does she recognize or include the therapist. The therapist accepts Linda's silence and does not pressure her into verbalizing her feelings.

In the third session, Linda repeatedly questions the therapist about the play materials and their use. She seeks support continually from the therapist. She uses diverse strategies to get the therapist to do things for her. She avoids making decisions or taking the responsibility for her behavior. The therapist conveys his understanding and accepts her feelings, while at the same time encouraging Linda to make decisions for herself, to act on her own interests and preferences.

Linda pretends at first not to recognize the rubber knives in the playroom. (Her mother had reported that she had a tremendous fear of knives.) Linda later expresses a desire to take a knife home.

Linda's anxiety returns as she struggles to decide whether or not she should paint and how she should paint. She continues to approach the items in the playroom cautiously and tentatively. Her insecurity and self-doubt are expressed many times in her attempts to get the therapist to make decisions for her.

Toward the end of the session, Linda decides to paint. Now her behavior reveals why it has been so difficult for her to get started. Behind her diffuse fears are strong feelings of anger. Once she starts painting, Linda's mood is freer. She is able to disclose her anger. She paints various pieces of the doll furniture with red paint and expresses a desire to drown "them," the family doll figures, in the red-painted and red-soaked bathtub. She spills water onto the floor, stomps around in it, and forcefully swings two rubber knives in the air as she moves wildly around the room.

Fourth and Fifth Play Sessions with Linda

Play sessions four and five repeated the core themes of the third session. Immersion into the splashings of red paint dominated her behavior. Anger and fear, approach and avoidance characterized both her play constructions and her interactions with the therapist. At the same time, in these sessions, frequent moments of positive communication with the therapist occurred as she invited him into her play fantasies and conveyed her feeling of security with him.

Sixth Play Session with Linda

In the sixth session, Linda continued to develop a growing freedom and trust in the relationship therapy. She made decisions quickly and acted spontaneously. She showed much more confidence in her play, frequently saying, "Because I want to." She engaged in a vacillating battle between expressions of hostility against people and a desire to be accepted and valued by them. In a sustained episode, she worked on her fear of knives. She also threatened at one point to cut the therapist. Later, unconcernedly, she moved the knife blades freely across her hands.

C: (*Runs into the room and goes immediately to the pail of water, shouting.*) I'll throw it right on the floor! I'll put it right on the rug! (*Spills water on the floor.*) So there. So there.

T: All over the floor, and near the rug.

C: Yes. I'd like to stomp it all over your face.

T: You'd like to stomp it on me.

C: (*Walks to the vise and touches it.*) Open this for me. I can't do it.

T: You can't do it, hm?

C: Nope.

T: (*Opens the vise.*)

C: I teased you. Goody, goody, goody.

T: You teased me, hm? You could have done it all the time.

C: (*Laughs.*) You found out.

T: Mm-hm.

C: I'll stomp you with this.

T: You really want to stomp the water on me, but I cannot let you do that.

C: Why?

T: You just may not do that here.

C: (*Laughs loudly.*) Then I'll stomp in it, and I don't care if I get all wet. Hey! My sock is wet. I'm gonna throw some more water on the floor. (*Takes pail into bathroom and enters with it filled with water.*) I'm gonna spill it all over.

T: There, it splattered all over.

C: (*Laughs.*) Let 'er splatter all over. Lock the door. Lock it for me.

T: You want the door to be locked, hm?

C: Yes. You do it for me. No one can get in here. I'll splash them if they try. (*Steps around in puddles of water. Then goes to dollhouse.*) I'm gonna move the house. I'm gonna put it right in the water.

T: Right in the middle of the water, hm?

C: Yes. I'm gonna put it in the water. And if somebody comes up this chimney, they'll put the stove on real quick, and they'll go right in it.

T: Right into the fire and get all burned.

C: (*Picks up a toy table.*) Who broke this?

T: Who could have done that?

C: Well, I don't like it. Everything is getting broken, and I won't fix it. Whoever broke it, they'll fix it. (*Picks up pieces of doll furniture and places them in different rooms of the dollhouse.*) We'll have two bedrooms and two basements. And the bathroom goes right in there, doesn't it?

T: Wherever you want to put it.

C: And here's the kitchen, and the toilet.

T: Mm-hm.

C: And this is the room when company comes. Company could go to this company house, couldn't they?

T: Mm-hm.

C: And this is for play. This is the playroom.

T: So they have a playroom, too.

C: Yes. And up here they can put the sick people. (*Suddenly stops. Picks up a knife.*) I'll cut you—cut you to pieces.

T: You want to cut me, hm?

C: Yes. I'll cut you if you talk to me.

T: You don't want me to say anything else, or you'll cut me.

C: Yes. I'll cut you. Cut you wide open. (*Stares at therapist a long time, then drops the knife. Continues to furnish house.*) Here's a table.

T: Mm-hm.

C: You said something! I'll shoot you.

T: You not only feel like shooting me, but you are going to shoot me.

C: Yes. Because I want to. You said something, so I'll shoot you.

T: If I talk, you'll shoot.

C: Yes.

T: You're sure about that.

C: Yes. You said something! I'm going to shoot you, and I'll cut you up.

T: You'll cut me right up, hm?

C: Yeah.

T: That's what you feel like doing.

C: Yeah. (*Puts a few more pieces of doll furniture into the house, leaving considerable space in each room. Then walks away from the house and moves to the vise.*) I'm gonna take this apart. (*Laughs as she takes vise apart.*) Goody, goody.

T: There, you took it apart, and you're glad.

C: (*Picks up a gun. Goes to the dollhouse and starts shooting at it.*)

T: Bang.

C: (*Shoots gun four more times.*)

T: You shot four times.

C: No, I'll shoot eleven times. (*Continues to shoot gun.*)

T: Eleven times.

C: Yes. Because I wanted to. (*Drops gun and continues to furnish dollhouse. Then goes to clay and starts pounding it with her fists.*) I'll paint this clay.

T: You only have a short while longer left today, Linda. Then we'll have to stop.

C: (*Shouts loudly and angrily.*) Why?

T: Because that's all the time you have.

C: I won't go! I don't want to go back there. Not ever.

T: You don't want to go back, hm? But that's all the time we have.

C: Why? Why? Why? Why? Why? (*Pause.*) Here. Open these. (*Hands therapist paint jars.*)

T: Pretty hard to do, aren't they?

C: (*Returns paint jars to workbench and picks up a balloon.*) What's this doing down here?

T: It's just there for however you want to use it.

C: (*Picks up jar of blue paint and pushes up her sleeves.*) I'm gonna paint with my hands. I'm gonna paint the whole floor. (*Pulls out paints and paints the floor. Then takes a piece of paper and makes patterns on it with finger paints.*) I'm gonna take this back to school with me, because I did it, and I want it. (*Pause.*) I wish you'd move all these things out and have them in nursery school over there.

T: You'd like to have them all over there, hm?

C: (*Rubs paints all over her hands.*) There. Cake. Cake.

T: Making a cake, hm?

C: Yes. Put clay in it and get it all over my hands. I'll paint the clay. I want to take this picture home.

T: When it dries I'll bring it to nursery school, and then you can take it home.

C: I want to take it home now.

T: It's too wet to take now. Well, Linda, your time is up. We'll have to stop for today.

C: No! I won't come!

T: You have to come now.

C: When—when I—when I come, you have to stay here all by yourself. You have to stay here for a lotta weeks. You never can go and eat or anything.

T: You want me to just stay here all the time, is that it?

C: Yes. I'm gonna wash my hands. I'll wash them right on the floor here. (*Rinses hands in water on floor and starts to splash the therapist.*)

T: No, Linda, you may not splash me with the water.

C: Why?

T: Because I won't let you do it.

C: Well, I'm going out here to wash my hands.

Discussion

In this session, Linda almost immediately expresses feelings of resentment. She focuses her feelings on the therapist, wants to splash water around him and throw water in his face. She tricks him into opening the vise, laughs in his face, and screams, "You found out."

When Linda is told she will not be permitted to continue to throw water at the therapist's face, she becomes dependent and passive for a while. She finds a way to express her angry feelings, throwing water all over the playroom and stamping around in it. She wants the playroom door to be locked and threatens to splash anyone who enters.

Later in the session, Linda's behavior changes. She expresses positive feelings in her play with the family figures. She furnishes the dollhouse, using all the rooms and leaving space for company. This is in contrast to her earlier behavior of cramming every piece of doll furniture into one small room of the house.

Linda's anger returns and is again directed toward the therapist. She shouts at him, threatens to cut him wide open, and warns him that she will shoot him if he talks.

From this point to the end of the session, Linda fluctuates between shooting at the dollhouse and family figures and creating a comfortable home atmosphere.

Realizing that she has but a short time left to play, Linda becomes upset and hostile again. She paints the playroom floor and screams at the therapist. The negative feelings are shorter in duration and more moderate in intensity than previously. Linda proceeds to finger paint, working spontaneously and freely. Toward the end of the session, she shows self-regard, as she refers to her painting and says, "I'm gonna take this back to school with me, because I did it, and I want it."

Eighth Play Session with Linda

Linda continues to express hostility against people in her play. Violently punching the comeback clown, she attacks the figure repeatedly. In the last half of the session, her behavior fluctuates. First, she calmly builds a house. Later, she destroys it, calls it a "dummy-bum house," and scatters the block pieces everywhere in the room. At the end of the session, she paints joyfully and with pride in her creation.

C: (*Walks into the room and goes to the doll figures. Laughs.*) How many dolls here? Seven. (Laughs again.) Look. I broke one. (*Removes the head of the mother figure.*)

T: Mm-hm. You broke one, and you don't care.

C: (*Takes all the clothes off the doll figures.*) I'm gonna throw all the clothes in the water. (*Throws clothes into pail of water. Then picks up a dressing table and places it in the dollhouse. Opens roof of house.*) Look. They can walk into that room and that room and through here. They have fun. And they can look out the window. They can go up and down. (*Pause.*) I'm not gonna furnish their house up.

T: You're not going to furnish it, hm?

C: Nope. Not for anyone! Just throw it in there. (*Throws the family dolls into the dollhouse.*)

T: Throw them right in, hm?

C: Yes. Everything. And I don't care.

T: You don't care what happens.

C: Yes. I don't care if anyone gets broke. I'll just throw them in there anyway. (*Picks up a toilet and places it in dollhouse.*) They can walk into the bathroom and out through there. (*Stares at dollhouse for a while.*) Look. It's funny. A funny house.

T: Mm-hm.

C: I'm making it that way because it is that way.

T: You're making it funny because that's the way you feel about it.

C: Yes. (*Pause. Points to the comeback toy.*) Look at him. He's a clown with two faces and two heads.

T: He's an old smarty.

C: Yes, he is. (*Picks up a balloon and squeezes it.*) I'm gonna bust this balloon into pieces.

T: You'll rip it apart, hm?

C: Yeah. And make them all bust.

T: You'll make them all bust.

C: Yes. (*Throws balloons into pail of water. Runs to comeback and hits it in the face.*) I smacked him. Gave him a good smack.

T: You got him right in the face.

C: Goody! Now I'll finish him up. I'll throw water on it. I'll drip it all over him.

T: You're really going to get him all over.

C: Yeah. (*Hits comeback several times, first in the stomach, then in the face. Pulls comeback around the room.*) I'm going to make him go all the way down to the floor. I'll punch him right in the face.

T: You'll really bust him.

C: And I'll make his eyes go away.

T: And then he won't be able to see.

C: No, he won't. But I will. (*Splashes water all over comeback and shouts.*) You big old dumb-bum! (*Pulls comeback toward pail.*) Now I'll stick his head down in the water.

T: You'll smack him right down there.

C: He's a dummy. He's a dummy. I'm gonna throw the water all over the whole place.

T: You want to just throw it everywhere.

C: Look what a mess. There, I gave it to him. (*Pushes comeback down to floor and jumps back with a frightened look as comeback starts to rise.*) He can't get up, can he? He can't get up.

T: Are you afraid that he might?

C: (*Laughs. Splashes more water on the comeback.*) He got it again. Right on his head.

T: Right on his head.

C: I'm gonna pour the whole thing on him.

T: Mm-hm.

C: I'm gonna step on him if he don't lay down.

T: He'll either lay down or you'll step on him.

C: Yes. Now I'll make him dirtier and dirtier. (*Breathes heavily as she pushes comeback and hits it. Watches it come up slowly and then pushes it down again. Tries to keep comeback down by putting part of it under a table.*) Stay down! You stay down! You keep him down. I'll put the chair beside him. There.

T: He's lying down now.

C: (*Picks up pail of water and throws water on comeback. Walks around, stamping in water, and chants.*) Dumb-dumb-dumb. Dumb-dumb-dumb-dumb. Dumb-dumb-dumb-dumb. Dumb-dumb-dumb. (*Throws remaining drops of water in pail on comeback.*) I'm going out and get some more. (*Fills pail with more water from bathroom.*) He's gonna get splashed again.

T: Yes. You'll give it to him again.

C: I'm gonna throw it on his eye first.

T: You really splattered him.

C: I splattered him all over. (*Drops pail and walks to box of blocks.*) Now I'm gonna build him a house. And my house is gonna be bigger than ever. Why do you have the blocks?

T: You wonder about that.

C: For no one to play.

T: They're not for anybody, hm?

C: No. Just me.

T: Only you. No one else. No one but you.

C: No. No one but me.

T: Mm-hm.

C: (*Finishes building a house of blocks.*) There. This house is a dummy-bum.

T: A dummy-bum house.

C: Yes. Because they're dumb.

T: Mm-hm.

C: (*Picks up blocks and throws them against the wall. Laughs very loudly.*) I almost hit that.

T: Yes, you almost hit the mirror, but I cannot let you throw blocks at that.

C: (*Starts to throw blocks into pail of water.*) I'll throw them in the water. Look. I hit it. Hit the pail.

T: Mm-hm.

C: I'm gonna take all the blocks and throw them right in there. (*Picks up the masks. Tries them on and laughs as she puts each one on.*) Now I'm gonna play with this piece of clay. (*Pounds clay on table.*)

T: Linda, you have only a short while longer to play.

C: (*Puts some red paint on the paper. Then covers whole sheet with red, yellow, and blue paint.*) Look. Look what I made.

T: Mm-hm.

C: Is my time up for today?

T: You only have a couple of minutes left.

C: Why?

T: That's all the time left.

C: Because I have to go back to school. (*Makes another painting, using all three colors.*) See? I'm making this here.

T: Mm-hm.

C: There. It's finished. Can you bring my pictures when they're dry?

T: You like what you've made?

C: Yes. You put them up to dry and bring them to me later.

T: All right, I'll do that. Your time is up for now.

Discussion

Linda begins this session by expressing anger and resentment, possibly toward her mother, removing the head of the mother-doll figure and laughing loudly. She does, however, also express positive feelings in her play. Using family figures, she throws all their clothes in water. Then, she lets the family explore the "spacious" house and indicates the numerous conveniences they have. Linda becomes resentful again and exclaims, "I'm not gonna furnish their house." She throws the family dolls into the house and says she does not care what happens to them. Linda wants to "bust the balloons into pieces." She hits the comeback toy in the stomach and face a number of times, and expresses a desire to blind "him." The comeback toy may represent her father, who has been critical of Linda and frequently calls her "dumb." Linda retaliates with, "You big old dumb-bum!" She repeats this again and again and then sticks "his head down in the water." When the therapist wonders if Linda is afraid he will strike back, Linda laughs and splashes more water on the comeback toy and holds his head under the water, shouting, "dumb, dumb, dumb."

Later in the session, Linda's feelings toward "him" are more positive. She says, "Now I'm gonna build *him* a house. And his house is gonna be bigger than ever." However, she becomes ambivalent again and is uncertain whether the house is a good house or a "dummy-bum" house. Linda spends the remaining time painting and proudly asks to take her paintings home.

Linda's experiences in play therapy may be summarized as follows: Her initial attitudes were characterized largely by negative feelings and intense anxiety. As her anxiety lessened, a form of generalized anger appeared. At first, the anger was directed toward the therapist but later toward the mother and father. As more and more of the negative feelings were expressed and explored in the therapeutic relationship, positive feelings began to emerge. At the end of the eighth session, as evidenced in her painting creations, Linda was more valuing of herself. She enjoyed and liked what she did. She also was more accepting of her parents. Unfortunately, Linda had not fully worked through her anger and her ambivalent attitudes toward her family.

The school staff reported a considerable change in Linda's behavior, and her mother indicated that a number of positive changes had occurred at home. After her third play session, the school notified the therapist that Linda was beginning to play with other children. For the first time in her two years at nursery school, she told a story to the children and led a group of children in a number of dance movements. She no longer spoke in a whining tone; she was more decisive and free in her play. Her teacher said that Linda was participating in discussion periods. She was surprised, too, that Linda was joining others in the dance activities. Her teacher also reported that now Linda had two friends in school with whom she played frequently.

In conferences with Linda's teacher, sometime after her eighth session, it was reported that the above changes had become even broader, and that Linda was much happier in school. Her teacher stated that the most outstanding difference seemed to be that Linda was expressing her preferences and making choices. At home, she was a much less frightened child, more sociable, and more considerate of others in the family. Unfortunately, Linda's mother abruptly ended the play therapy sessions.

Carol

Carol, an only child, 4 years old, was referred to the play therapist by a community agency. Mrs. L, Carol's mother, worried about Carol's recent complaints of stomach pains during mealtimes. Also, Carol's habit of twisting and pulling her hair had become so serious that she had become partially bald.

Family background data included the following: the mother's repeated statement that Carol looked and acted like the mother's stepsister whom she hated, the mother's rigid standards on cleanliness, and the degradation she had experienced in her own family. Mrs. L's stepparents had been alcoholics. She reported that her childhood home was usually littered with scraps of food and dirt. Carol's parents emphasized that she was incapable of loving them or anyone else. The seven-room family home was shared with three other families.

Mrs. L was seen regularly by a caseworker. The play therapist had two interviews with her. The first of these was held before Carol's first play session. After the final play session, a second interview was conducted. Highlights of Mrs. L's attitudes toward Carol, as expressed in the first recorded interview, follow.

> I can't accomplish anything with her. She just won't listen. You have to use force. You just can't treat her nice and expect to get results. . . . I punish her frequently, and then she becomes a very, very good girl, but it makes me feel like a worm afterwards. But then she just can't understand anything but that kind of treatment. . . . She's just very selfish, and that's all there is to it. What makes me so mad is that she's so quick to notice when someone else is selfish, but she herself is a selfish person. . . . She just seems to be getting worse and worse. . . . She's pulling her hair out all the time, and she always complains about her stomach at meals.

Mrs. L also described Carol as inconsiderate, disagreeable, and unruly. The therapist found her to be a frightened, lonely, love-hungry, confused, and angry child. Carol had twenty-one play therapy contacts. During this time, she frequently expressed resentment, hatred, loneliness, and fear.

Intense feelings against her mother were prominent in these sessions. Carol struggled to free herself of emotions that tortured her. Gradually, she came to see herself more clearly as a good person. She understood how her relations with others might improve. Initially, she spoke in a language that the therapist did not understand. As the play

therapy process unfolded and the child–therapist relationship deepened, Carol expressed herself clearly. After the fourth session, Mrs. L
reported that Carol's stomach pains had disappeared. Through play
therapy, Carol began to respect herself and others. Excerpts from the
recorded play sessions follow.

First Play Session with Carol

> (*Mother enters the room with Carol.*)
> M: Isn't this lovely?
> C: Mm-hm.
> M: Do you like this?
> C: Mm-hm.
> M: Now you play down here. O.K.?
> C: Mm-hm.
> M: Then I'll go see Mrs. D. O.K.?
> C: Mm-hm.
> M: All right.
> C: Mm-hm.
> M: And I'll come back and get you. O.K.?
> C: Mm-hm.
> M: He's going to watch you, darling. O.K.?
> C: Mm-hm.
> M: O.K.?
> C: Mm-hm.
> M: O.K.?
> C: Mm-hm.
> M: Do you want to kiss Mommy? (*Kisses Carol's cheek.*) O.K.?
> C: Mm-hm.
> M: I'll be back. O.K.?
> C: Mm-hm.
> M: All right. Bye-bye.
> C: Bye.
> M: (*Walks out of the room after looking back at Carol.*)

Throughout the session, Carol constantly refers to worn toys and as the hour ends remarks, "I guess the kids don't break 'em. I guess the people who bring 'em in just break 'em first and then let the kids play with 'em."

Second Play Session with Carol

C: I'm gonna use this stick to paint with.

T: You are?

C: Mm-hm. I'm not messing up my hands. I'm gonna use all of these.

T: All the colors, hm?

C: That's what I'm gonna do. Use all of them. That's what I always do. (*Pause.*) We have much troubles. Much troubles.

T: You really have troubles, don't you?

C: Mm-hm. I'm gonna wash my hands.

T: You don't like your hands dirty.

C: I don't much. No, I won't wash my hands now. I'll wait before I go upstairs.

T: Before you go upstairs, hm?

C: I don't want my mommy to see them dirty.

T: You don't want her to know about it.

———•———

C: (*Picks up nursing bottle and chews on the nipple. Drinks for a while and then starts chewing again.*) Looks like I'll have to stay here nineteen years.

T: A long, long time.

C: Just for this old bottle.

T: That will keep you here.

C: Yes. (*Laughs and continues to drink. Chews nipple for quite a while.*)

T: Just keep chewing on it, hm?

C: My mommy is going to have to wait until I get to be four years old.

T: She'll have to wait until you grow up to be four, hm?

C: Yes. (*Sighs heavily and continues to chew nipple.*)

C: I'm gonna shoot up this whole place.

T: Just shoot everything, hm?

C: Yeah. (*Laughs shrilly.*)

T: Shooting all over.

C: (*Laughs.*) I'm shooting everybody in the place. Everybody except my girlfriend.

T: She's the only one you won't shoot.

C: Yeah. I'm gonna shoot you now. (*Laughs.*) Why don't you fall down?

T: You'd like me to fall.

C: Uh-huh. After I shoot you, you can stay up just one minute. Then you be dead. (*Shoots at therapist and laughs.*) You don't get up.

T: Not ever get up.

C: You never get up. Nobody's gonna see. I'm gonna shoot the lights off.

Discussion

Mrs. L seemed anxious and needed reassurance before leaving Carol with the therapist. During the first session, Carol chattered incessantly. She pointed to the toys but did not play with them. She appeared to be unsettled and restless.

Carol characterized her home as a place filled with troubles and her mother as someone to be feared. She drank from the nursing bottle and chewed the nipple, saying, "My mommy is going to have to wait until I get to be four years old." Her negative expressions became more generalized. In her play she shot all the humanlike figures in the room, except one doll which she identified as her girlfriend. She was especially vehement against the therapist, shooting him and telling him to die and never get up. At the end of the second session she shot at all the lights, so that no one would see the "crimes" she had committed in her play.

Fourth Play Session with Carol

C: (*Designates an area while playing in the sand.*) That stuff you see is halfway up to the north.

T: Halfway up to the north, hm?

C: Yes. And this north has a monster. The other north has nothing in it except trees.

T: Nothing but trees.

C: The other north is wild.

T: Two norths. A wild one and a peaceful one.

C: You can get lost in it. You could get lost all over 'til you go straight. Then you could get to the cars. You get to the cars, and then you walk a little further, and then you get to my farm. You got a driveway going up there. Way up on the hill.

T: Mm-hm.

C: Yes. Mine's way up there on the hill.

T: Your farm's up high?

C: No. I changed it to a house.

T: Just changed your mind.

C: Ain't it looking perfect now? This is where the seeds grow. And they're gonna grow up, and stuff is gonna be all around here. Don't you see? Don't you see the house here?

T: Mm-hm.

C: And there's going to be stairs going up here.

T: I see.

C: And this is going to be a room right through part of the house. This was the rough place, but you can pat it right down like this. It's a house. It's a house. Don't you know?

T: It's a house.

C: It's a house. Not a real toy.

T: It's a real house.

C: Yeah. The whole thing is big. It's all one house.

T: Mm-hm.

C: And this house is gonna storm now.

T: Really going to storm.

C: Many years ago it stormed down.

T: It was all broken down then.

C: Yes. You see, this part's gonna come off.

T: Tear right down.

C: Just this part. Just the roof.

T: Mm-hm.

C: And there's a safety zone down here to save the people. The people come down to here after the storm. Then they come back here and build it up again. Then the storm comes again and blows it away. Then the people come and put it up again.

T: Mm-hm.

C: This part here is gonna be a secret panel so the people will never know what a big house.

T: They'll never know the truth about it.

C: That's right. At night is when the storm comes up, and then comes the morning, and then they can build it up safely so that it won't come down again.

T: Mm-hm.

C: It all looks different now.

T: Not the same any more.

C: Don't you know what happened in the storm? It all fell. This is gonna be a special one. She didn't like the other one, and she never will.

T: She never liked it.

C: It'll be all zoomed up here. You wouldn't like *your* house to fall. Well, the storm—. She must have got the bad lady. Her didn't like anybody except the house cooker.

T: She liked only the house cooker.

C: Mm-hm. Who cleaned her house. She didn't like the strange people. They got her then. They got her right down, and that was the end of her. No. That wasn't. That was the end of the people.

T: All of them died?

C: Except the good ones. It all happened years and years ago.

T: Many, many years ago.

C: That's when I was a baby. And the storms came and tore everything apart. Now the whole thing's crashed down. (*Stands back
and surveys sand pile.*) I'm all done with that. That finishes that
job. (*Picks up clay and flattens two small pieces of clay.*) Everything's always the same.

T: Nothing ever changes here.

C: I have to shine my glasses. *Some* glasses she gave me. I'm gonna
tell her this is no good. It's not even glass.

T: She gave you some pretty poor glasses, hm?

C: I'll take 'em back. They're not even glasses. There. Now listen, I
want some good glasses back. (*Pretends to open a package.*) Same
old glasses!

T: She's given you the rotten ones again.

C: I'll take them back and see what she'll give me this time. Oh, lookit.
Oh, oh, how pretty shined they *look*. But they're still the *same* old
thing.

T: You've been cheated so many times, haven't you?

C: I'll take them back. Now let me try these. They look shiny. But
they're no good.

T: Every time they look so good, and they turn out to be so bad.

C: Well, *this* time she gets some good ones. Now what is she going
to have for lunch? (*Continues to play with the clay.*) Half a motor-
cycle and a little butter. I guess I'll wrap it up. She told me that
I'd like it. If you don't eat it, you're gonna get a licking. Let's see
if this would be butter. Oh, it should be. It's good work stuff. Aah,
gee, that's supposed to be butter? That's butter I'm getting? Oh,
I hate it, I hate it. Turn it over. Mix it up. Are you gonna eat it?
I wouldn't. What's it supposed to be? Now he'll find out what he's
getting. But he won't like it. She sure don't fix his lunch. She fixes
it the rotten way. He's gonna fix his own, and he won't fix another
rotten one. This man sure is a good kind. Good as gooder. (*Pause.*)
Oh, this tastes so good. Now I'm gonna kill some of this clay if
she don't know any better. She sure gave me some rotten stuff.
I'll see what she says about this piece. If you couldn't eat it, then
you can't. Let's see what she says about this stuff that she wanted.

If she do that again, she'll get some bad. Oh, what she does! One slice she gives. One slice and one slice and one slice. Oh, I hope you got the good food you wanted. Do you want good food? You're getting it. Here, I'm giving it away. She won't like it but she gives mine away, and I don't like that. It's a good thing you're sitting over there, because I don't want to get any cutting on you. (*Looks at therapist.*) You might get cut open.

T: I might just get cut open if I weren't over here.

C: Mm-hm. Might get cut and ruined. Do you mind if I wrap it up and throw it away? I don't want it any more.

T: That's up to you.

C: She'll find out it was me.

T: And are you afraid?

C: She gave me dumb. Well, she's gonna have dumb right back.

T: You'll give it to her right back, hm?

C: If she gives it to me again, she's gonna get it right back.

T: You mean you'll give it to her if she does it again?

C: She will. You should hear her when she starts. She started it years and years back.

T: It all started a long time ago.

C: Yes. Now see what she says about this stuff. She's not gonna like it.

T: You won't let her get away with it, hm?

C: She won't never get away with it with me. I'll tie her up and say that I'm moving.

T: If you have to, that's what you'll do.

C: I'll move even if I don't have to. I'll move anyway. (*Picks up small nursing bottle and sprinkles clay with it.*) Squirt, squirt. I'm gonna squirt her. See how she gets it now.

T: She's getting it now, hm?

C: She will get it. She won't like it the way I'm gonna fix it. She'll get it the same old way.

T: You'll give it to her just like she gave it to you, hm?

C: Because I don't like hers. I won't eat her food. I'll eat the other people's food. Their food is better.

T: Her food makes you feel bad.

C: I'm gonna cut her open and see her. Here's your old sicky food.

T: You'll cut her right open and give it back to her.

C: She'll say, "Ah, what kind of food is this?" And she'll say, "That's good; it must be good." But it won't be.

T: If she says it's good, it probably won't be.

C: Probably I'll put poison in it. I'll put it in it.

T: Poison in the food.

C: Yeah. And if she says it's good, she'll find out. How you like this food? It won't make you die. This will be much gooder. Some of this is so good. And some of it's got poison in it.

T: Some is good and some is bad, hm?

C: She'll say it's all good when it isn't. And she'll eat it. Aah! I'm dying. Thought it was good food. Some good food you called it. Rascal food. Now I'll put some good food in it. Some real good stuff. I'm gonna cut her open and get all that bad food out. And put some good food in. It's good food, but she thinks it's poison. She thinks she's dying. She's just making herself dead.

T: She thinks she's dying and making herself dead.

C: Mm-hm. She won't be. She'll be alive as anything. This is good food. I'm getting hungry as could be, so I better eat this good food that I got her. Wow! I'm afraid! I hope I don't die.

T: You're afraid to eat the food, is that it?

C: No, thank you. Now I've got a good bite to eat. So I guess I'll go on to the good part. (*Runs back to play in the sand.*)

Discussion

Carol expresses a range of strong emotions in this session. She creates two norths, a peaceful one and a wild one, which may represent her ambivalent feelings toward her own home situation. She makes a house in the sand, destroys it, builds it again, and destroys it, reenacting this play sequence a number of times.

Carol's despair and loneliness seem very great as she looks at the therapist and says, "You wouldn't like *your* house to fall." She conveys the emptiness of her emotional life and attributes it to the fact that "she must have got the bad lady," who didn't like anybody and was interested only in cooking and cleaning. Carol indicates it all happened when she was a baby, "and the storms came and tore everything apart."

Carol's anger becomes direct as she reveals how her mother has deceived her and cheated her. Her feelings are intense; her sarcasm mounts. She expresses her extreme resentment of her mother, who always tricks her and withholds her love. In the play situation, Carol retaliates by poisoning her mother. Later in the session, Carol shows the positive side of her feelings, understanding her mother's desire to be loved. She takes "all that bad food out" and gives the mother good food.

Fifth Play Session with Carol

C: (*Kneels in sandbox and builds with the sand.*) Four years ago a rock—a rock felled on this house. So we call it a part of the house.

T: Four years ago a rock fell in it?

___

C: (*Plays in the sandbox.*) She turns it up herself, and she plays all around and has a lot of fun. That's the way it should be. She used to laugh, but not Mama.

T: She laughed, but her mama didn't, hm?

C: Her mama used to holler all she could. She'd holler and holler and holler. All she wanted was a house. Not a big house. Just a little girl's size.

___

C: (*Plays in the sandbox.*) Now she says it looks like a house. She screams out, and ever since she's crying. It's different, this house. First the daddy left the mother, and now the mother left the daddy.

T: Mm-hm. Daddy left Mommy and Mommy left Daddy.

C: So you know what she did? She built herself a house her size. She crashed down their house to make her own house.

T: She made a house all her own.

C: Nobody lived in it except her, and everybody's happy now. Except her. So she's cut hers off again.

T: She didn't want her house attached to theirs.

C: So she moved it down to California, and they didn't like it. But she loved it. And she brought water for her house. A little water. Water in a tub for her house. All around the house, water, water, water. And her house is bigger. And her house is bigger and bigger and bigger. Finally she wanted it hooked on again. So you know what she did? She moved again and hooked hers on. So they were glad. And their family wasn't happy, and she was happy. Before, they were happy and she wasn't happy. So what's the difference?

T: She's happy now, and they aren't.

C: So she crashed her house down again and made another one. If they wanted to hook on, she didn't mind.

T: She would let them hook on, hm?

C: Only how could they hook on, the way thay had built it?

Sixth Play Session with Carol

C: (*Builds large mounds in the sand.*) I want to be warm. It's rock cold.

T: Cold as rock.

C: Colder than rock.

T: Mm-hm. Quite cold.

C: You'll never know.

Seventh Play Session with Carol

C: (*Sits in front of the dollhouse and plays with doll figures.*) My hands are ice cold. What kind of water is this? It's so cold. Turn on some hot water. No. We don't have any hot water. But there *was* hot water. It *was* hot water. It's just so cold. If you do what I say, you can get out of there and have hot water. *Now* do you understand? So they had to do what she said.

T: They have to do what she says in order to get warm water.

C: They can't do what she says. We're stuck in with glue. Too bad we can't. Be quiet, they shout. So they did be quiet. They can't hear my noise, but they can hear their noise. See what they did? They told you to get out of the house. Now get out! And I mean get out! (*Pause.*) Finally. But—hey, hey, it's cold out. It's cold out anyway. Be quiet yourselves. This house is not for big people like you. So she took a gun and shot them one by one.

———•———

C: (*Still playing with doll figures.*) They're so cold here. Even the horses had to go outside. It's lucky they had a heater. But she got colder and colder. She just couldn't stand it. She just couldn't stand it.

———•———

C: (*Handles clay at workbench.*) I guess I'll put on these aprons. Aprons, aprons, aprons. Guess I'll put on two aprons, because I'm gonna get awful dirty. (*Picks up scissors and jabs at clay.*) Zhoop, zhoop, zhoop, zhoop, zhoop, zhoop. Oh, goody! She's stabbed. She used to think about this stuff that was good. She used to dream about it. So Mommy could fix it up so she liked it. How did she dream about it? How did she used to do it? She used to say, "Give me the porcher [the good food], the porcher, porcher. Give me the porcher, porcher." Boy! Was that ever good!

Eighth Play Session with Carol

C: (*Plays with doll figures while sitting in front of the dollhouse.*) She calls them good, only they're bad. Because when Mom calls them good, *she* calls them bad. Mom calls them good, but she calls them bad. They don't agree. (*Pause.*) Here's another one that she likes. But Mom says this one's bad too. And she likes the bad ones.

T: She likes the bad one, does she?

C: Mm-hm.

Ninth Play Session with Carol

C: (*Plays with the clay and the vise.*) I'm gonna smash it in two. Wanta see me smash it?

T: You're going to smash it in two, hm?

C: (*Pushes the clay into the vise.*)

T: Carol, you have only a short while longer to play. Just a few minutes more.

C: A few minutes? I don't care about that.

T: Just a few minutes.

C: It's long enough. Isn't the Fourth of July long enough? It's long enough. I have to grind this up now. (*Puts more clay into vise and handles it for a few minutes.*) I'm through. Can't stay here all day. Next time I come, I'm gonna do it backwards. Start with the clay, then the dollhouse and the sandbox.

T: You know exactly what you're going to do.

C: And after that I'm gonna start with these balloons.

T: You've got it all planned out.

C: Yeah. I started it all.

T: And now you're going to finish it.

C: Mm-hm. It's all in pieces now.

Discussion

Carol dramatizes the loneliness of her life. In her play, "she used to laugh," but "her mama used to holler." She makes a house in the sand "all her own," is happy and satisfied at first but soon becomes dissatisfied and unhappy. She is uncertain. She is afraid to love her parents. In her play, she fluctuates between moving away from them and staying near them, exclaiming, "If they wanted to hook on [to her house], she didn't mind." In earlier play sessions, Carol was determined to move away permanently.

"My hands are ice cold," she screams, "she got colder and colder. She just couldn't stand it. She just couldn't stand it." To be cold, for

Carol, is to be distant, isolated, detached, and lonely. She holds the adults in her life responsible for her unhappiness.

She expresses hostility toward adults in her play, shooting all the adult doll figures one by one.

Carol plays out her conflicts with her mother numerous times and shows how strongly they disagree. As the ninth session ends, she becomes decisive, knowing exactly what she wants to do: "Next time I come, I'm gonna do it backwards. Start with the clay, then the dollhouse and the sandbox. And after that I'm gonna start with these balloons."

Through the play therapy meetings, Carol has developed an increasing self-confidence and a clarity about who she is, how she feels, what her interests are, what she wants to do—a gradual but vivid shift from uncertainty to decisiveness.

Tenth Play Session with Carol

C: (*Plays with the clay and vise.*) You put this in here. This is the last time I'm getting into this. This is the only time. Then I'll forget about the whole thing.

T: Mm-hm. This is the last of it then.

C: I don't care about cutting. I just care about the clay.

C: (*Still playing with clay.*) Squawking all the time. I don't like that.

T: You don't want that, hm?

C: Squawk, squawk. That's all they figure. They just can't help it. Squawk, squawk. That's all they can, squawk. Squawk, squawk. That's all they'll get back. If I don't get it, then I won't give it. I get squawk, squawk. Something else. That's what I'd like. Something else.

T: You wish they'd give you something besides squawking.

C: Talk, talk. Squawk, squawk. That's what they do. I'll put a snake in there. See if that squawks. I think the snake does. Water snake, water snake. You go in there. I'm home, snake, and my mama won't let me go out any more. Squawk, squawk. Squawking all the time.

Eleventh Play Session with Carol

C: All you do is sit, sit, sit. Well, I don't want you to do anything more.

T: You feel that that's enough.

C: Just that and nothing more.

Twelfth Play Session with Carol

C: (*Plays with doll figures at the dollhouse.*) Everybody's going to be naked in the family.

T: A whole family without clothes.

C: Then the boys can see the girls, and the girls can see the boys.

T: Each one can see the other.

C: And I can see all the little children with their clothes off. And then they're gonna take *all* the people's clothes off. Not just dollies. All their clothes are gonna come off. The children will see each other.

Thirteenth Play Session with Carol

C: (*Plays with the clay and paper towel.*) I think I'll wrap this up for lunch today.

T: That'll be your lunch, hm?

C: Yes. I guess I'll have this for us to eat. I got it all wrapped up. He *only* has to go to work. To work, to work, to work, to work. She bothers me every day. (*Pause.*) It's so quiet around here today. That's what I want. Just so much peace and quiet.

T: That's what you want most. Just peace and quiet.

C: Because the old mother hollered at me every day. Hollered every day. And all she wants is peace and quiet.

C: No home. No home at all.

T: Not a real home, hm?

C: No house like you have. Like kids have.

T: You don't have a house like other kids, hm?

C: No. In mine it's just the same old things. All I do is walk around and do nothing. That's all I can do.

T: Just walking around with nothing to do.

C: I'll stop now. I'm going upstairs.

Fourteenth Play Session with Carol

C: (*Plays with clay at workbench.*) Look. What a silly. What I'm doing! I'm cutting.

T: You're cutting and being silly.

C: No. I'm not silly. Now, I'm having good things to eat. And I'm selfish. I don't want anyone else to eat my things. (*Pause.*) Do you want something to eat?

T: Do you suppose that I would?

C: Yes. You might like this to eat at home.

Fifteenth Play Session with Carol

C: (*Plays with the clay.*) You know, I live alone.

T: All by yourself, hm?

C: But I have two sisters who live down the street. We fight once in a while, but we get along most of the time. (*Pauses as she fingers clay.*) I don't like boys. They're nasty.

T: You don't like boys.

C: Well, really *they* don't like me. Maybe I'd better go back to work. I'm gonna have lunch. Would you like to eat with me?

Discussion

Carol again expresses feelings of anger and resentment toward her parents. In her play she refers to their constant quarreling and indicates their frequent criticisms of her. She retaliates with "Squawk. Squawk. Squawk. That's all they'll get back."

Later Carol removes the clothing from all the doll figures and implies that if all people were "naked," we could see each other as we really are.

Hostility toward her mother reappears. Carol wishes to escape her mother's persistent admonitions. In a whisper she says, "It's so quiet around here today. That's what I want. Just so much peace and quiet." She describes the tragic nature of her home situation, telling the therapist that she has no home at all, not like other kids.

As the sessions continue, Carol becomes more relaxed and spontaneous in her play. There is even a childishness about her. In previous sessions she has acted more like a miniature adult. She is often silly now and laughs frequently.

Carol recognizes her selfishness but justifies it, indicating that she has never had good "food," but now "I'm having good things to eat." When her feelings of selfishness are accepted, she offers to share her "food" with the therapist.

Sixteenth Play Session with Carol

C: (*Plays in the sandbox.*) They're gonna have a new house. I think this house is a music house. Ha ha, a music house.

T: That's what. A music house.

C: It's going to be so big that they're gonna have to put some music in this house. They'll have to have a television too. They're gonna crowd the house.

T: They want to crowd the house, hm?

C: But I'll fix it. That piano goes out farther. I'll put it back a little.

T: Mm-hm.

C: All right. A nice little room. How do you like it? Don't it look nicer with the piano spaced out farther?

T: More space there, hm?

C: And in here we'll have a door. It's gonna be a little hideout. And the kids can see their mother at night. And the kids can fool their mother. But the big people—they can just see from the top. And if the mothers go through there to the hideout, then—bang. The whole house gets on fire.

T: That's what would happen, hm? The whole house would catch fire.

C: Now the kids are gonna build themselves another house. And their mothers.

T: Just for the kids and the mothers, hm?

C: No. Just for the kids. And it's gonna be just right.

Eighteenth Play Session with Carol

C: (*Plays in the sandbox.*) And then she dreamed another story.

T: She dreamed another story.

C: This is gonna be the whole story she dreamed. She read it in a book once and said, "I'm gonna try and dream it." Then she thought maybe I should get a record of it first and see if it's scary. I don't like anything if it's scary.

T: You don't like scary things, hm?

C: No. I don't like cowboys and shooting. And even animals, if they're big. Every time I hear a noise when I'm up in bed, then I'm scared.

T: When you hear noises while sleeping, you're really afraid, hm?

C: Also when I'm bad sometimes and have to sit in a chair.

T: Oh, when you're bad and hear noises, then you get frightened.

C: Yes. When I hear noises then I'm always scared. My mommy comes and says she doesn't hear them, but I do.

T: You hear the noises even though your mommy doesn't, and it frightens you.

C: Yes. And it's really only something like the washing machine or somebody pounding.

T: It turns out to be something just silly, but it still frightens you.

C: Yes. It rolls me back.

Nineteenth Play Session with Carol

C: (*Plays in the sandbox.*) This isn't a free country. Nobody gets free here. But I made this. I made all my people, but I didn't make them right.

T: You made them, but they didn't turn out the right way.

C: I know things that they don't know. Ha ha ha.

T: You know some things that they don't.

C: This is my girlfriend. She likes me, and I like her too. I'm gonna eat my pie with her.

T: You like her, and so you're sharing your pie with her.

C: Yes. We'll eat it. She gets half and I get half. She thinks it's too much for me, but I've been starving to death, so I'll eat it. (*Pause.*) You know, kids just love people, but sometimes people don't love kids.

Twentieth Play Session with Carol

C: (*Plays in the sand and describes the destruction of a village by a huge storm. The people work together to rebuild it.*) If I helped them, then they'd like me, and it will never be crashed again. I'll make a great big cake for them. How deep is my cake gonna be? Oh, my cake, cake, cake. Baking a good, delicious cake. No, I'm gonna eat it all up.

T: Just for you, that cake.

C: Not all of it. I'll divide it up with them, because they're my friends. Friends, friends. *I'm* a friend, and I'm not gonna eat it all. I'm gonna give them some.

———•———

C: (*Plays in the sandbox.*) A lotta times she dreams about castles. She dreams about all this, only it's too late now.

T: Is it too late for her now?

C: Well, maybe not. I'll make one for her. I'm gonna make the castle. I'm gonna make Carol the first castle she's ever had.

T: You're going to do that for her, hm?

C: Yup. And tonight it's gonna be filled all around with pretty water.

———•———

C: See this cake? You can cut it in many pieces. In small pieces for many people.

T: That's the way you want to cut it, hm?

C: The big chiefs get the biggest pieces. Yes, the biggest chiefs always get the biggest pieces.

Final Play Session with Carol

C: (*Plays in the sandbox.*) Nobody knows what I know. Nobody knows what I know. (*Chants.*) Nobody goes where I go. Nobody wants to go where I go. Nobody wants to go where I go. (*Pause.*) You take the dirt, and you take the water, and you mix it together. Water and sand. Rub it, squeeze it, mix it. That's what you do in here. You mix things the way you want. I'm gonna make *some* pie, I am. And then there won't be any more time. I'm gonna make a pie so big it's gonna cover the whole place up. The biggest pie you ever saw. There's my pie. And now I'm gonna cut it up in little pieces and share it with all the people. We'll all eat it now.

T: It's time to leave now, Carol.

C: G'bye.

T: Good-bye, Carol. It's been very nice knowing you.

Discussion

These sessions are filled with Carol's expressions of positive feelings toward herself and other people. She builds a music house with blocks, where children are close to their parents. She plays games and creates a spacious house where "the kids are gonna have a good time."

Carol describes her fears of large animals and loud noises and recognizes that the fears are foolish.

In the twentieth session, Carol creates a village in the sand. She decides not to destroy the homes this time. Instead, she realizes that "if I helped them, then they'd like me." She makes a huge cake in the sand and decides at first to eat it all up, as her "selfish" feelings momentarily return, but later she exclaims, "I'll divide it up with them [all the people], because they're my friends." She now sees herself as a friend, someone people care about and regard as important. For Carol it is not too late; her dreams can still come true.

Carol brings the play therapy experience to a close, aware of her own powers of self and creation: "I'm gonna make a pie so big it's gonna cover the whole place up . . . and now I'm gonna cut it up in little pieces and share it with all the people."

In earlier sessions, Carol had expressed deep resentments and fears in her relationship with her mother. She was able to talk about her fears that the food would be poisoned, that her mother gave her bad food and little love. She had been cheated many times but she also recognized the concern and caring of her parents. They began to hold a more realistic place in her life. Acceptance of herself and her mother enabled Carol to move out of her angry world and express feelings of affection and friendliness. Many of these positive feelings and explorations were dramatized in her play in the sand. Carol expressed a desire to help people, to do things for them and with them, and to win their friendship and their love.

In the therapist's first contacts with Carol's mother, she described Carol as selfish, inconsiderate, disagreeable, and unruly. In the last meeting, she commented, "It is not very difficult to see Carol's growth. For a long time now we have had to punish her very little. Her manners are improving. She just seems to do things much better. She seems to just get along better with everyone. . . . My husband says she's been acting a lot smarter and has noticed lately that she's using big words when she speaks. . . . I think sometimes when I look at some other people's children that Carol is almost perfect. . . . For four years of her life, Carol showed us very little affection, but in the last six months she has begun to kiss us and to hug us. My husband is much warmer to her now, and he spends much more time with her. . . . Last night she said,

'Dear God, please don't let there be any more trouble between my mommy and daddy,' so it shows that she does have a great deal of consideration for us."

With this final meeting, the play therapy with Carol came to a successful ending. She has remained with me throughout many years and will always be a vivid reminder of what it means to a child, to be in a loving relationship and member of a loving family.

7

Play Therapy with Families

*I*n contacts with families, I have consistently emphasized attitudes of faith, acceptance, and respect. Whether a request for child therapy has come from an agency or from a parent, I have responded in a timely way. When parents have believed, at least initially, that the child is at the root of family problems, I have accepted their interpretation. When they have made mistakes in child care, I accept these errors. Parents are often bewildered by sudden changes in a child's behavior, such as the onset of terrifying fears or temper tantrums.

Faith in parents' ability to grow in their understanding is an essential condition of relationship play therapy. This value is conveyed to them throughout every contact. In relationship play therapy, parents are invited to come for therapeutic help and to participate in interviews focusing on their child. Before beginning play therapy, an interview is scheduled with parents. The therapist listens empathically and creates an atmosphere of openness, trust, and acceptance.

Sometimes a parent leads the interview with a discussion concerning the child and later focuses on herself or himself. At times, parents will state that some other member of the family is primarily responsible for the child's difficulties. Or, they may concentrate on an elaboration of the child's symptoms and how the child's behavior is affecting family living and school relations.

At the end of the initial interview, time arrangements for play therapy are completed. Parents are invited to participate: "If you'd like to meet with me and share your experiences with your child, or anything else, either on a regular basis or as needed, do not hesitate to contact me."

Parents commonly request counseling help when they perceive that the therapist is interested in and respects their views. Of ten cases of child therapy handled over a period of nine months, four parents requested counseling for themselves, five decided to call me when they felt a need for consultation, and one decided there was no need for contact with the therapist, except to receive progress reports. Typically, these parents also focused on their own personal lives and relationships, rather than solely on their child's problems.

When parents request information on their child's progress, a brief review of the play therapy is offered. Omitted are the child's personal stories, belonging only to the child. In meetings with parents, the relationship play therapist responds primarily to the parents' feelings, and provides child development information when that is what the parent needs.

In arranging the child's play therapy experiences with parents, permission to record the play sessions is requested. The one-way-vision mirror in the playroom is explained to the parents, as well as the fact that a person who records the interviews, and sometimes students in training, are in the observation room. Occasionally, parents ask to observe their children from behind the mirror. Here a limit is set, and it is explained that this would violate the values of privacy and confidentiality and would be unfair to children to observe them without their knowledge.

Occasionally, children insist that their mother join them in the playroom. When this happens, the child's decision is accepted and the parent remains in the playroom for the entire first session, or as long as the child requires the parent's presence. The presence of the child's mother, for example, does not impede therapeutic movement. In some ways, her presence facilitates the play therapy process. In addition, the parent has an opportunity to observe and learn from the therapist's communication and interactions with the child.

To illustrate relationship play therapy when members of a family are involved, I have selected my work with a preschool child and her family. Abridged recorded transcriptions of my interviews and discussions of the major issues and outcomes of therapy are presented.

Therapy with the Bernard Family

Mr. Bernard contacted me by phone and spoke with urgency and distress: "I want to come and talk to you as soon as possible. It's my little girl Kathy. She suddenly seems to be afraid of things. A month ago she woke up one night with a horrible nightmare, and this had continued for three nights in succession. Her fears don't seem to go away." One day Kathy's mother read her a story about a chicken falling upside down in the air. Kathy screamed with fear and wanted the book destroyed and thrown away. Kathy's mother, Mrs. Bernard, continued, "Now there are some things in every book which she is quite upset about. She wants them all destroyed. One day Kathy saw a billboard sign and started crying. She was afraid of the picture." Kathy did not want to stop long enough to hear her mother explain the billboard. Then on their way home they saw the same billboard again. Her mother said she had made a mistake and gone by it a second time. Kathy cried for two and a half hours afterwards. Mrs. B added, "We thought she'd never stop. She wakes up and has nightmares. She is terrified. I want to know what I can do about it, for if it's developing into something, I wouldn't want it to drag on too long."

Following this telephone conversation, arrangements were made to meet with Mr. and Mrs. B and their 3-year-old Kathy. Over a period of approximately eight months, Mr. B met with the therapist four times. He made numerous phone calls both between interviews and after completion of the last interview. Mrs. B also saw the therapist four times. Fourteen play sessions were conducted with Kathy. Since Kathy refused

to come to the playroom without her mother, the sessions were conducted with both mother and child, and an attempt was made to establish and maintain a therapeutic relationship with each of them during
the play sessions.

As the work progressed, Mrs. B herself encouraged Kathy to make
decisions, she responded more and more to Kathy's feelings, and accepted her choices and the consequent behavior.

October 25. Interview with Father

T: Feel free to begin wherever you'd like, Mr. B.

F: Actually, my wife is the one that should be able to talk about it,
because she's been with her more. I put her to bed at night. I like
to do it, and Kathy doesn't mind it. It seems to us that she has a
fear, and naturally she can't tell us, and we can't diagnose it. We're
so ignorant we can't handle it.

Let's take last night. She talks for a while. She talks about things
to herself. At three o'clock this morning she woke up. I used to
be a heavy sleeper. Now I wake up at the slightest sound. She was
a preemy and was eight months old and was 3 pounds 4 ounces
at birth. She's very healthy, and there is nothing wrong with her.
When she woke at three o'clock this morning, we found her whimpering. My wife picked her up and brought her in our bed. We're
just completely stymied. After she was in our bed for five minutes,
I said to Kathy, "Would you like to go in your own bed?" and she
said "No," and I said, "You tell us when you want to go in." We
waited, and I asked her again several minutes later. We felt we
shouldn't force the issue, because maybe she wanted to be with
us more. Finally, she said, "O.K.," and she went into her own bed.

After she was in bed, I said, "I will sleep in the bedroom with
you." Kathy didn't fall asleep right away. I was just falling asleep
when I heard her say she wanted the bedspread all on her. I tried
to explain to her that it was too big on the bed. I got out of bed,
because Kathy started to cry again. I held her hand and touched

her body, and she kept whimpering and sniffling. I gave her a little pat on the back, and she sniffed and lied quietly. I stood there and looked at her, and she asked me why I was looking at her. I have noticed several times before when I told her, "If you want to cry I will give you something to cry about," she would stop crying after I patted her. Our pediatrician said she probably had a fear complex. She fell asleep, and when I went to work this morning she was still sleeping.

(*Pause.*) I don't know whether this is normal, farfetched, or what. This billboard deal last Saturday—I want to tell you about it. I had Kathy with me all day. She had told me, "Don't go down——— Road." No sooner had we turned the corner, and there was a bill-board showing a woodpecker pecking on the tree. She immediately told me that I had promised I wouldn't go down that street. She threw herself on me and started to tremble and cry. I held her and tried to explain about it. She kept saying, "Tear it up—get rid of it." I tried to explain it is not our sign, we can't tear it up.

Maybe we shouldn't have gone into detail with it. Maybe we've always gone into too much detail with her. If I were to tell her a story, she would interrupt me and ask why. If I made a definite answer maybe she wouldn't go any further. After I talked to her, she finally calmed down to some extent. I said, "Probably some people own the sign," and I said, "Maybe we can see them and ask about it." Then she smiled. As we went down ———Road, she said, "Don't go that way." It all ended up where she forgot about it, and we went to my cousin's house, and that was the end of that. Now, Doc, tell me what I should do to get rid of that fear.

T: There isn't anything specific you *should* do. I have no suggestions. However, perhaps if we continue to talk this out, a solution may become clearer. Also, if you'd like, Kathy could come here for play therapy sessions, which will give her an opportunity to fully express herself in her own way.

F: Now that doesn't make any sense to me. I came here so you would tell me what to do.

T: And I'm telling you that there isn't anything that you *should* do.

F: Well, there must be someone I can go to who will tell me what I should do.

T: You want me to just say to you, "Do so-and-so, and so-and-so, and so-and-so." Is that it?

F: Well, not exactly, but I do want you to tell me what to do.

T: Tell me more about your relationship with Kathy.

F: The first time I noticed this fear was when my wife was reading a story to her. She noticed a duck falling, and she became terrified about it. She said, "Take it away—tear it up," and my wife took the book and threw it out. Then Kathy seemed to be satisfied, but later she asked, "Did you throw it out?" That was the end of that incident.

During the day she plays well. So you see, we just don't understand. I know you can't solve this in five minutes' time, but still there must be something that you can tell me to do.

T: You just can't handle it any more.

F: It might have come on a long time before, like when I took her to the zoo when she was two. We were standing in front of the animal cage, the tiger, and she was trembling, and I walked away at that time. Before that, we used to live on——Avenue. Next door there was a little girl older than Kathy. Kathy looked up to her, but this girl treated Kathy very mean. Another time Kathy went to take a dog, and the dog snapped at her.

When we go out for a ride, I suggest we sit together, and we do many things together. We sing together, and so forth. As a matter of fact, Kathy has learned the words to all the popular songs. We live a fairly normal life. We have a home. I have a secure position. We don't bicker. If there is a disagreement, we'll hang off until Kathy is in bed asleep. (*Pause.*) I have an idea that I should have stopped at the billboard and walked up to it with her and then say to her, "Touch the bird." Any intelligent person will know whether that's right or wrong. (*Pause.*) I hit her last night, because I thought she was just fooling around.

T: You felt that maybe she was deliberately trying to irritate you, and you were angry.

F: You hit on a point there. Kathy doesn't let a thing pass. She is a very sensitive child. You just touch her, and boom—tears. Maybe I show anger where I am not supposed to. She can read every angle on my face.

I wish you would talk to Mrs. B. My wife is very easygoing—a patient woman. I would trust her with my child more than any other woman on earth. To me, she is a very good mother. Maybe she could throw some light on all this.

T: She might help us understand the difficulty a little better.

F: I was here at two-thirty, though I knew the appointment wasn't until three. This was silly, and yet I had to get away from work, with the thought or feeling, "Maybe I am doing something wrong."

T: You feel that you might be to blame for it, then.

F: If my own life means anything—. My real mother died when I was born, and I was placed in an orphanage at the insistence of my stepmother. My father remarried shortly after my mother died. Seeing that, my grandmother couldn't see me staying there, so she took me to live with her. I hadn't seen my parents or brothers and sisters at all. Then when I was 12, my sister suddenly came and got me from my grandmother's, and then I lived with them.

I can remember a couple of instances when I was terrified. My two uncles had an argument over which way to paint the side of the house. One uncle wanted to fight it out, and I can remember sitting on the curb just frightened, seeing them fight it out.

My stepmother, not being too intelligent and not able to read, favored my sister and more or less didn't care about me. There was such a complete change from my grandmother's home that I was practically alone. I felt that I wasn't wanted. It seems to me that I have felt very insecure most of my life, but I married someone who has all the love and kindness for me and who gives me everything I need, yet I'm not really happy.

T: In spite of your relationship with your wife, you still feel insecure.

F: I feel safe to say that I am pretty well set in my life. Going from me to Kathy about that insecurity, maybe I am transferring it to Kathy. When I come home at night I pick her up and kiss her. I ask her how she is and kiss and hug her. When I do that, maybe I speak in too rough a tone, and she may be afraid. I don't know whether it is a feeling of sorrow or a feeling that I wish it could be done away with.

T: Whether you feel sorry for her or consider it a weakness in her.

F: What's disturbing me is the fact that she's got the fear, and maybe it's deep basically.

T: You're afraid it might be deeper than just the fear she shows.

F: Could you see Kathy? What did you call it? Play something?

T: Yes. I could see Kathy for play therapy sessions. I would suggest that you tell her that she's coming here to play. I would also like to make an appointment with your wife before Kathy comes in.

F: You know, I can't remember a single thing that you've said to me, but somehow I feel better than I did when I came in.

October 30. Interview with Mother

T: You can feel free to begin wherever you'd like, Mrs. B.

M: I am sure Kathy doesn't know how it affects me. I will tell you what I remember. Just yesterday I was driving down the street, and we saw these sign boards. The eyes bother her all the time. One is a fruit, and there is a big eye on it. She throws herself down in fright. I try to avoid it, but she always finds it.

The other night she watched singing on TV. It was a Halloween program. There was a fire and a ghost in it. We turned the set off as soon as the fire and ghost appeared, but she saw it and she talked six hours afterwards about it. We took her to the dime store, and she saw masks. Now we can't go in the dime store any more.

Now I have to sleep in the room with her, or my husband does. Another thing, she is afraid of the dark. (*Pause.*) She used to be Daddy's girl. I don't know what happened. One night they were lying down and he had his back to her, and something happened, and ever since then she feels that way.

T: You can't remember exactly what happened, but you feel that that was quite an important incident.

M: I just can't remember what took place that night. She loves him. She kisses him. Since this stuff started she doesn't behave as well as she used to. She is very negative. She used to sit down and read books for hours. She used to sit down and enjoy the books. She's afraid of the "Big Bad Wolf." She now won't look at her books. One by one she rejected all her records. First it was the "Big Bad Wolf," but then it generalized to everything.

Here's something else. We moved to a new neighborhood, and the girl next door is quite aggressive. My daughter is a big girl, and if she ever kicked someone, they'd really get hurt. We finally got her so when someone hit her, she would hit back. But now it gets to the point where she often starts the hitting, and sometimes she'll want to fight all the time.

She is indefinite about things. If I offer her a sucker, she'll say "The green one—no, the red one—no, the orange one" and keeps changing her mind, so I offer her two. Do you think that's all right?

Another thing, I don't know if this is unusual. She had a favorite blanket. One day she kept saying, "What's this? What's this?" It was a label on the blanket. About three days after that, she said she didn't want the blanket any more. That's the first thing that she said she didn't want. The other day she said she would use the blanket after the label was taken off, so I cut the label off. We're in a quandary. I don't know whether I should curb her or whether I should just let her do it.

She loves fur. This is something else. She wanted me to buy this fur muff. The thing had two tails on it. She told me I would have to take the tails off. I had to cut the tails off before she would use it. Anything she doesn't want—"Tear it up—I don't want it—get rid of it."

She's not too shy. She knows all the popular songs. She always tells us to tell her kitty [the muff] what she doesn't like to hear herself.

I can't go on——— Road. I can hardly go anywhere. She looks for it. She's under the strain because of the sign. It isn't the sign. It must be something else. If she sees anyone with their eyes closed, she becomes frightened. If someone closes their eyes to think, then she doesn't like it.

I know the signs and not going to bed drives us crazy. She used to like the dark. I put the night light in her room. She used it about two weeks and was crazy about it. One night, she sobs to herself when she wakes up and doesn't find us there. She'll hold us real tight after we come in but not tell us what it is. The other night we took her into bed, and after she was in it a while I said, "You have to go in your room now." I turned her bed around so it would be parallel to mine. She talked about the train, which was really a reflection from her night light. She is afraid of reflections. While lying in our bed she saw a reflection from the bathroom light. She keeps yelling on and on and on, "Take it away!" I had to throw the night light away. She used to say, "I don't like that. Give it to Donna. I don't like the night lamp. Give it to Donna."

Let me ask you something. As far as my husband's home life and mine, we never fight. We never argue in front of our daughter. I never nag. If he wants to go out bowling or someplace, then he goes. There is never any argument. We never bicker or argue. But there must be something. Maybe she could be jealous about our relationship. (*Pause.*)

Our daughter means the whole world to us—both of us. Apparently we do something wrong. We do feel that it is probably us, but I can't see it. Nothing has changed. I guess we've drawn the conclusion that it is always the parents from what people tell us. My sister-in-law voiced the opinion that we were teaching her too much. She's such a well-spoken child. Could she be angry because everyone tells me how good she is?

T: Evidently you feel that might anger her.

M: Suddenly it occurred to me that this is possible. When we go out, she performs better than anyone else. We went to a birthday party just a while ago. She sang a number of songs and entertained the people. We always have felt proud of her. We compliment her a lot. I read someplace to tell the child it was well done. Maybe she has too much of a strain on her.

T: You mean you might expect too much of her.

M: Let me ask you something. I took many of the TV programs that she used to watch away. Just an innocent program might frighten her.

She is perfectly fit physically, and now we have to have this thing on us. She doesn't go into tantrums when she is terrified. She just whimpers and sobs quietly. Something else—if she is doing something and you touch her the wrong way, she gets real tense, and she'll say, "Put it back."

Everything must be just right for her. My cousin gave me a blue skirt for Kathy. I tried it on my daughter, and now she wears that skirt continually. She won't put anything else on. I washed the skirt, and even before I have it ironed she wants to put it on. She has all kinds of dresses and skirts and slacks, but all she asks for is that blue skirt. She won't wear her royal blue dress. She won't wear slacks any more.

I let her know when she's done something wrong. I really believe there is something in the relation with my husband. Now she doesn't want her daddy to put her to sleep. She wants me to do it. If I'm not there, though, she'll cling to her dad. If he can get her in the right mood even now, she'll let him put her to sleep. When he picks her up now, she tenses. Her daddy—whenever she does something, he wants her to do it just right. Her daddy always tells her what to do. She'll say, "No, I want to do it like this." Then he leaves her alone. I don't notice that he's done that so much. I just happened to notice it just yesterday. He calls me forty times a day. After he talked to you, he was fine. He is being exceptionally sweet to her. No child could want a better daddy. He doesn't correct her too much.

What do we do when my husband and I don't agree on the treatment or something? It happened yesterday, but I can't remember exactly what the incident was. However, sometimes when she

wants to eat out of a blue dish rather than the one I've set before
her, or if she wants a flowered glass, then I'll give her that. Should
I do these things? My husband doesn't think so, but I don't think
it makes any difference. What do you think about it?

T: Evidently you get somewhat worried when your husband disagrees with you.

M: My husband and I have been married nine years, and we have
never really quarreled. We just don't do it. Everything has been
wonderful. We never argue in front of Kathy, though if I do something that he thinks is wrong, he tells me about it in a way that
she doesn't know about it, but maybe she has understood all these
times and we didn't know it. Maybe she has been sensitive to this.
Tell me—will you be able to correct these fears?

T: There is no definite way I can answer that. It will depend on
whether or not Kathy and I can work out the kind of relationship
that will enable her to express herself freely. . . . If you would like
to come in yourself, either regularly or from time to time, just to
talk things over, you can let me know.

M: Right now I can't tell you. I still don't feel too good about this
whole thing, but if I decide that I want to come and see you, it
probably will only be from time to time.

November 1. Play Session with Kathy and Mother

T: (*Shows Kathy the bathroom.*)

C: I'm not thirsty.

T: You can use these play things any way you like.

C: (*Walks into room with T, then runs back into hall to get Mother.
Mother sits on chair and C runs out to hall again. Carries in small
chair.*)

T: Kathy wants to bring in her own chair.

C: (*Looks at Mother while holding chair.*)

M: Put it down.

C: I wanna make toys, Mama. (*Picks up truck.*) Mama, how do you work this? What's this, Mama?

M: That's a dish.

C: Here. (*Hands mother a ball, balloon, dish, and truck. Continues giving mother play materials.*)

M: Thank you.

C: This is a hoe. You got a hoe. I like the hoe. (*Hands mother a tractor.*) Here, Mama. (*Pulls chair closer to table and sits down.*) A boat. A hot water bottle, if I wanta. (*Picks up gun.*) This is a gun. (*Looks at T and continues to handle toys. Picks up telephone.*) What's this? (*Hands mother a rubber knife.*) Here's a knife for you. That's a sharp one.

M: Mm-hm.

C: You can cut, Mama. (*Handles the gun again.*) Here's a gun. Here, Mama. Lookit this gun and shoot. (*Hands gun to mother.*) You shot me.

M: I shot you?

C: Yeah. (*Kathy takes gun and shoots mother. Hands T the little miniature gun.*)

T: You want me to have this? O.K.

C: Now quiet. I'm gonna talk. (*Holds a large telephone and turns dial a few times.*) I'm dialing and dialing. Hello. Hello. Who's there? Mama, you use this one and I'll use that one. (*Hands mother large telephone and takes smaller one for herself.*) What's this, Mama?

M: It's a steam shovel.

C: What does it do?

M: It picks up dirt.

C: (*Handles telephone again.*) I'm gonna call up. Hello? Who's there? Nobody's there. (*Replaces telephone on table.*) Here's an airplane, Mama. It flies.

M: Mm-hm.

C: And here's an automobile. And another car. (*Moves to doll furniture and doll figures.*) Here, doll. Sit on the couch. Another doll. Look, Mama. She's got her pajamas on, Mama.

M: Mm-hm.

C: Here's a bed. (*Continues to handle doll furniture. Picks up wash-stand and examines it. Handles part of the steam shovel. Looks at cat balloon on floor and then at mother. Picks up balloon and carries it to mother.*) This is a heavy balloon.

T: A real heavy one.

C: See what color it is. What color?

M: Purple.

C: Purple. (*Gives mother the balloon.*) Here's another balloon.

T: You want Mama to have all the balloons. Just piling them all up on her.

C: Fly the balloons up in the air.

M: I can't. My hands are full.

C: (*Picks up small washing machine.*) What's this?

M: You know what that is.

C: It goes around and around. Turn it.

M: I can't. My hands are full.

C: (*Hands T the washing machine.*) Will you do it?

T: It's very hard to turn, isn't it? There.

C: (*Holds washing machine. Sits next to blocks and handles a few of them. Goes to doll furniture and picks up rubber doll.*) Take the diaper off and wash it.

M: I can't. Ask Mr. C if he will help you.

C: I'll stick myself with the pins.

T: Is that what you're afraid of?

C: Yes.

T: (*Removes pin from doll's diaper.*)

C: (*Places diaper in washing machine.*) Make it wash.

M: Honey, I can't. I'm too loaded down.

C: (*Places washing machine on floor.*) It's washing.

T: And you're getting it all clean.

C: (*Sighs heavily. Sits on floor and watches washing machine.*) It's turning.

T: Mm-hm.

C: Around and around and around.

T: That's the way it goes.

C: (*Looks at large comeback toy.*) What's over there with the hands? (*Goes to comeback and lifts it.*)

T: You could lift it right up.

C: (*Carries comeback around floor to mother. Places it in front of her. Goes back to washing machine.*) Look, Mama. It's washing. It's gotta get dry 'cause it's dirty. Now stand over and let it wash. (*Picks up bells from table.*) Jingle, jingle, jing. Jingle, jingle, jing. (*Picks up miniature hammer.*) Mama, this is a hammer. What do you hammer on?

T: On anything you want to.

C: I can hammer on—so. (*Hammers on bells.*) Is there a big hammer down here?

M: I don't know.

C. Who wants to hammer? Who wants to hammer? (*Hands T the hammer.*)

T: You think I want to have that.

C: Here's a gun. (*Hands mother the gun. Picks up small doll.*) Baby gonna go swimming. That's what I was looking for. What's this, Ma? [*Small balloon.*]

M: It's a little balloon.

C: How did it get little?

M: I don't know.

C: You can have that balloon.

M: Thank you.

C: You can have the pretty balloon. (*Hands balloon to T.*) What fell? (*Gives mother blue gun that has fallen from her arms. Picks up small nursing bottle.*) Here, Mama. For you. And I'll take the big bottle.

T: You'll take the big bottle and Mama will have the little one.

C: Is there a doll I can feed, Mama?

M: Look around and see if there is.

C: (*Picks up rubber doll, places it in her lap, and feeds it with large bottle of water.*) Now drink. Is the water coming out? I need a big baby, Mama. I need a big baby. I really need a big baby. I need a real heavy baby. I've got a big bottle.

T: You need a heavy baby.

C: I need a big baby. I gotta have a big baby—a heavy one. Mama, is there one like that?

M: I don't know.

C: I'm looking for another one. Mama, is there any big ones down here?

M: Well, find something to feed.

C: I need a big baby. Mama, I gotta feed a big baby.

T: You just have to.

C: Mama, I gotta have a big baby.

M: Well, I just can't help you, honey.

C: I'll feed this one. (*Places small rubber doll in lap again.*) Now drink your bottle. Now drink your bottle. (*Glances at diaper in washing machine.*) It's washing. Look. Diaper's washing. Maybe I better put some water in it. (*Takes diaper out of machine and pours water into it. Covers it again.*) It's got to wash. It's got to wash.

T: It's got to get clean.

C: Why doesn't the water come out, Mama? It's supposed to. She changed her mind and she wants to have the other bottle. Give me the other bottle. (*Takes small bottle from mother. Feeds doll with small bottle.*) It doesn't come out, Mama.

M: It doesn't?

C: No. Can I take it off? [*Nipple.*] Mama, how do you open that big thing? How do you open it? This kind of open is easy. (*Refers to small nipple.*) Mama, why does it stay in the bottle? I want it to feed.

M: (*Laughs.*)

C: Oooooh. Look what happened. Look what happened. (*Looks surprised at water that has dripped on her thighs.*)

M: That's O.K., honey. You can dry in the car.

C: If I get my dress wet, I can wear my slacks?

M: Yes, you can.

C: Oh, it got on my slip. I'm not getting it on the chair any more. Drink it all up. Can you pour some more water into this bottle? Can you pour some more water in here? My mama's hands are too full. (*Hands T large bottle. Takes nipple off small bottle herself.*)

T: Let's see. (*Loosens nipple from large bottle.*)

C: (*Transfers some water from large bottle to small one.*) Gotta put the top on. Quick! Before I spill it. It's too much.

T: There's too much in there.

C: Quick! Before I spill. (*Replaces nipple on small bottle.*) Now she's got some more water. She wanted some more and now she's got more. She's real thirsty. Boy oh boy.

T: You like to feed the baby.

C: Yes. She almost drank the water out. See? (*Shows mother the washing machine.*) It's dirty.

T: It's getting washed just like you wanted it to. (*Pause.*) Kathy, you only have a short while longer to play today.

C: Did you see what happened? It got all wet. Mama, do you have another pair of clothes for me?

M: I've got blue jeans or slacks in the car.

C: Blue jeans. You want to put all those things down. I'll help you. (*Unloads items from mother's arms.*) I'm gonna cut. (*Picks up knife.*) Mama, what should I cut?

M: Look around for something to cut.

C: I don't see any crust.

M: I don't think there is any bread down here. (*To T:*) She doesn't like the crust on her bread, so we've been cutting it off, but lately she's been eating it. (*To Kathy:*) Don't you, honey?

C: I'm gonna cut some bread and butter. (*Gets into sandbox and plays with sand.*)

T: We have to leave now.

M: We'll come back again, honey.

T: This time will be saved for Kathy each week.

C: (*Gets out of sandbox. Walks out of room with mother and T, with a backward glance at the room.*)

Discussion

In the November 1 session, Kathy clings to her mother for a short while. She continually loads her mother with toys and play things even after her mother protests, "I can't. My hands are full." At one point, she shoots her mother with a toy gun but only after inducing her mother into shooting her first.

In her play, Kathy is restless. She engages in hyperactive movements, and exhibits anxious behavior. She constantly questions her mother, wants her mother to do everything for her and frustrates her mother by loading her down and then asking her to do things. Kathy seems to be angry with her mother but does not express this feeling directly.

Kathy is uncomfortable and unsettled in the playroom. She doesn't seem to know what she wants to do and moves about from one toy to another. She avoids the therapist almost completely yet is very much aware of his presence.

Kathy finally decides to feed the baby, and exclaims, "I need a big baby, Mama." She begins to play with continuity and persistence. There is considerable emphasis on cleanliness, as Kathy scrubs the baby's diaper again and again and shouts to the therapist "It's got to wash. It's got to wash." There is also a compulsive quality in the way she feeds the baby, "She's got to drink it. She's got to."

In a number of instances Kathy expects her mother to respond immediately to her demands and becomes angry when there is a delay. Toward the end of the session Kathy gets a little water on her slip. She becomes upset, asks for another set of clothes, and seems worried about being wet and unclean.

November 8. Play Session with Kathy and Mother

C: (*Runs into room and looks at toys on table.*)
T: Well, here we are now.
C: (*Picks up chair and carries it to table. Sits down and handles canoe.*) Here's a boat. Here's a boat. One for you. (*Hands T a*

boat.) And here's a boat for you, Mommy. Here, Mommy. No more. What's that? (*Picks up canoe paddle.*)

M: What does it look like? It looks like a canoe paddle.

C: I wanta play in the sand. (*Steps into sandbox and sits on ledge with feet in the sand. Plays with steam shovel in sand.*) Mommy, I'm gonna make you a cake.

M: O.K.

C: First a pie. Down, down, down. Downtety down. Down, down, downtety down. Down, down, downtety down. Mommy, I got myself dirty. (*Rubs hard at hands.*)

M: That's all right.

C: I'll brush myself off. (*Goes to table and picks up gun.*) Here's a gun like Donna's.

M: Mm-hm.

C: Shoot me with it. (*Hands gun to mother, who shoots.*)

T: Bang. Mommy shot you with the gun, just like you wanted her to.

C: (*Returns to sandbox. Hums.*) Here's yours. I made it already. Here.

M: Thank you.

C: Now eat it, Mommy.

M: O.K.

C: I'll wait till you're finished eating it. Are you all finished?

M: Mm-hm.

C: Mommy, the last time I played with water, and I got all wet.

M: Mm-hm.

C: Here. Eat it. (*Hands T a dish filled with sand.*) Are you all finished?

T: I'm all finished.

C: Give it to me. (*Pulls chair close to sandbox. Sits down and dangles feet over sandbox. Reaches down into sandbox for sand and grunts.*) You're gonna get this one.

———•———

C: Mommy's gonna get the green boat. Now Mommy's gonna get it.

T: Mommy's going to get it.

C: Yes. You had yours.

T: I had mine and that's all.

C: I just gotta have one once a day.

T: One once a day. That's all you need.

C: Yes. (*Hands mother boat filled with sand and watches her pretend to eat.*) What do you got in your mouth? Lunch?

M: Mm-hm.

C: (*Moves chair to table with toys.*) Mommy, sing "Red Red Robin."

M: You sing it, honey.

C: No, you sing it. (*Jingles bells while mother sings.*) Here's one for you. And you jingle that one. (*Hands a bell to mother and one to T.*) You jingle that. (*Goes to sandbox.*) I'm gonna make you a little jungle-ungle things. (*Moves from sandbox. Goes to dollhouse and furniture.*) Where's the washing machine? I can't find it. What's this?

M: What does it look like?

C: A washing machine. Where's the baby's diaper? Mommy, where's the baby's diaper?

M: Look for it, honey.

C: (*Looks in dollhouse.*) Where's the washing machine? Oh, here. Oh, I wish there was a fire. You better not go near there 'cause there's a fire. (*Shoots gun down the chimney of dollhouse.*)

T: Bang, bang, bang.

C: Shoot down this one. This mommy doll. She'll be burned by a real hot fire.

T: She'll be burned by a real hot fire.

C: (*Goes back to doll furniture and picks up toy lampshade.*) Look! A lampshade. This can go in there, too. (*Drops shade into sandbox.*)

T: Mm-hm.

C: Mommy, I gotta wash that now. Where's the baby's diaper? Gotta wash it. Unpin it. (*Hands doll with diaper to mother.*)

M: I'll unpin it and you pull it out.

C: Take it out. Here. Hold it. Mommy, I want this to wash. Make it wash.

T: You want it to be really clean.

C: Yes. This will go around and around and wash. (*Stuffs diaper into washing machine.*) It washes. It didn't wash good. It didn't wash good. Gotta look for another diaper. No more, I think. (*Looks over pile of doll furniture.*) Here's a toilet in case baby has to go make. Open it for the baby. (*Places baby doll on toy toilet.*) Baby make sissy. She's making sissy. She's making sissy. (*Places doll on stairway of dollhouse.*) Go right on the steps. Make it right on the steps. Wash and wash. Diaper isn't dry yet. Put some sand in here. Put some sand in here. (*Pours some sand into washing machine.*) Gotta wash. Get washed and dried. Clean up. (*Empties washing machine over sandbox. Bangs the washer against side of sandbox to remove all the sand.*) No more. Gonna wash now. It's gonna wash now. Gonna wash.

T: Your time is up for today.

C: Mommy, will you read me a story before we go? Read me a story.

M: O.K.

C: Hold my hand.

Discussion

Kathy's cleanliness anxiety reappears. She frequently looks at her hands and becomes upset. On one occasion, seeing sand on them, she rubs hard at her hands until every speck of sand is removed. Anger toward her mother is vague and tentative but definitely present.

Kathy begins to respond more to the therapist, moving back and forth from her mother to the therapist, giving him things to hold and making things for him.

Kathy's repetitive questioning continues. In the play, hostility toward her mother becomes more direct. She runs to the dollhouse, shoots down the chimney, and shouts at the mother doll. "Shoot down this one. This mommy doll. She'll be burned by a real hot fire."

Kathy searches for the baby's diaper and yells to her mother, "Mommy I gotta wash that now . . . gotta wash it."

She places the baby doll on the stairway of the dollhouse, saying, "She's making sissy. Go right on the steps." Kathy appears to be responding to everyday pressures related to cleanliness, dressing, and foods, pushing to grow up too soon.

At the end of the session Kathy mixes water and sand, becomes anxious on seeing the dirty water and walks over to her mother and holds her hand.

November 13. Interview with Mother

M: There are a million things I want to ask you. Her adenoids are very bad. They wake her up almost every night. She just lays there and can't breathe, and it terrifies her. One of us will try to quiet her, and it takes about two hours to quiet her. Will it hurt to have her adenoids taken out at this time? I haven't called the pediatrician yet to tell him. Her lips are continually sore and cracked.

She didn't get to bed until three o'clock last night. One of us has to stay with her every evening. She is terrified with everything in her bedroom. Now what can I do about it? I can just see the terror in her face. Finally I asked her what was bothering her, and she said she didn't want the linoleum in her room. But I don't think that's the solution, because then she wants something else destroyed. She made me paste something over the decal. Yesterday I had to cover up another one. She said she didn't like the animals in it. When she has to go to bed she is just terrified.

The day I called you to make an appointment we were really desperate. My husband had gone in to her, and he kept saying, "Why are you crying? Why are you crying? Stop it! What's the matter with you?" He is a very good daddy. He is not strict or anything. She wouldn't tell him what was the matter. I walked in and took her, and she came to me immediately. I held her for a while, and then I put her back in bed. My husband didn't sleep all night.

Next morning my husband called, and he heard her sing, "Far-away places, that's where I want to go." He got the idea that if he went away for a week, things would be better for her, but that night when he came home, she was so friendly to him he changed his mind. Usually he comes home in his work clothes. This time he came home with one of his good shirts, and she liked the shirt he was wearing. She clung to him. She wouldn't have anything to do with me. She insisted on him doing things for her. Everything was fine. Could it be the clothes he's wearing? Yesterday he was all dressed up, but she wouldn't do anything with him. He used to always put her to bed. She always preferred him, I told you.

She got over the sign boards. She doesn't cry any more. She is terrified by other sign boards now, but she doesn't cry like she used to. She just hides until we go by and then jumps up.

T: She acts differently but she's still afraid.

M: I don't know what to do, because she is increasing now. I think my husband should come down and talk with you. But he doesn't want to come. He figures he knows he is doing wrong, and we can't figure it out. He wants somebody to give him more direct replies than you do.

T: He wants direct answers.

M: (*Pause.*) It's gotten so that we don't agree. The other day her coat was lying on the floor. She wanted me to get her things. He brought it instead. She said to me she wanted me to bring it. He thinks I am catering to her. He doesn't agree with me. I was tickling her with her muff, and she enjoyed it. He considers it catering. He disagrees with me, and he'll make a remark about it.

T: There are things he doesn't think you should be doing for her.

M: If I feel like doing it, I do it. But my husband considers it catering. She enjoys it. Of course, he does the same thing, but he doesn't see it. He makes remarks, maybe a little remark here or there, and she'll catch it. It's been killing me, but I don't say anything until she's in bed.

T: You keep it to yourself, then, until Kathy isn't around, although it hurts.

M: If I say something, it's so she can't hear it. Yesterday something happened. She hadn't gone to the bathroom for a while. We never trained her. She trained herself. At 9 months she automatically began going herself to the toilet. For the other, she'd hear the older kids say "sissy," so she'd say "sissy," and then I took her to the bathroom. Now in the last four days she's really been resisting. I said, "You haven't gone for four hours. Daddy says you have to go before we leave the house." This was on Sunday. I thought I had tricked her into it. I got her upstairs and asked her to please go. I said, "You're wearing a big blouse like a big girl, so show me that you can go like a big girl." I said, "Don't you think you should go to the bathroom? Then there wouldn't be any trouble." I think there was too much of an issue made of it.

I feel it must be something that me and my husband are doing. If you could just tell us something—something to do with her. I wanted her to go to bed. Her face—she didn't want to cry. Now there isn't a thing in that room that doesn't terrify her. Let me ask you something else. If when she wakes up at night and she's terrified, would it hurt to take her into bed with us? I don't think that's a solution. I don't know what I've been doing. I've tried all kinds of things.

You know, what's wrong is we never had problems with her before. She always used to go to bed. She used to have a picnic. The books started the fears, then all records, then the signs. The whole process started. Maybe it started before then and I don't know about it.

T: It's just too puzzling.

M: Even up to now we haven't done anything. As far as my husband and I, we haven't changed. Maybe she's now seen something. Is that possible? This is the honest truth—my husband and I never disagree. We've never had a disagreement, never had a fight. *We have never really had an argument until a few years ago.* We used to take about two hours and pick each other apart about once a month, just for the fun of it. There was never really any criticism—there was so little. I don't know how to explain it. We used to say, "Get it off your chest." We're very, very compatible. Here's something, though. *We do disagree about my daughter now.* Like yesterday, she said something about the sign, and he was harsh, and I gave him a look. After we went to bed he said, "You didn't have to look at me like that."

She is such a darling child. She is so well behaved. She isn't any more. She lets you know when she doesn't like something. It bothers me that maybe it is something that won't be cured. Is that considered something mental? My husband and I are thinking of having another child. He thinks it would help her. She is very, very jealous. If some other child comes over and hangs on to me, she'll push his hand off.

My husband is just waiting for me to talk about Kathy's play each time she comes. Why is it when she leaves here, nothing registers? Here's what I wanted to know. Should we talk about her play here with her? My husband didn't understand. He said, "What did you do today?" I didn't think he should question her, so I told him it would be better if he didn't. He started to say, "Is that all you did today?" when she answered his question, leaving out her trip here. I changed the subject, and afterwards my husband and I talked it over. Can you ask me questions? Is there anything you want to know? Could it be a trifling thing? (*Pause.*)

I have been trying to make our family life perfect. Mother and Dad didn't get along too well. They used to fight and nag, so I always said I wasn't going to get married. Then when I grew up I said I wouldn't nag and I would always trust my husband. According to my husband, I think I have lived up to it. When he is late for dinner he'll come in and I'll give him a kiss and treat him just the same. I never question him. If he goes to the show with the boys, I would never say, "No, don't go," nor am I mad about it. Everyone who knows me has said I'm a very happy person. We live a perfect married life. I would never tell my husband that he does the wrong things.

T: You're very happy, and so you wouldn't tell him he's wrong.

M: It couldn't be just my husband, anyway. It could be both of us. Because right now she doesn't like him, he's sure it might be him. On Friday I was just desperate. He was all set to go away for a week to no place at all. He heard her singing over the phone, "I wish he'd go away for a week," and so he made a personal connection. But that night maybe she was sorry, because she showed him a lot of attention and affection. She didn't want him to hold her. She'd look away—she wouldn't look at him. The minute I came in, she held on so tight to me. I love her as much as he does, but I get a lot of joy in seeing her make him happy. I like to see her be Daddy's girl.

Here's something else I could tell you. When she's doing something, if he wants her to stop he'll pick her up and tickle her. He tries to get her to forget about it. Now he's trying to distract her too often, I think. When she is crying when she's with me, I don't try too hard to get her out of it. First of all, I don't think it would have hurt to let her play five more minutes with the toys. Instead of picking her up and making games out of it, and forcing her to bed, I would just let her play a little longer.

Here's something else. She always used to go up and down the steps. Now I've got to hold her hand. She'll stand there and she'll cry and cry and cry. Most of the time I will try to make a game of it. (*Pause.*)

T: Our time is up for today. Would you like to come in again next week?

M: Yes.

November 15. Play Session with Kathy and Mother

C: (*Runs into room and picks up bells.*) Mama. Mama, what do you do with this?

M: Anything you want to, honey.

C: Here's another one. Two jingles, two jingles, two jingles.

T: Two jingles up and down.

C: (*Holds bells in lap. Fills dish with sand and pushes bells into dish. Picks up spoon. Takes bells out of dish and digs in dish with spoon. Looks at mother.*) How do you do this? What do you do with it?

M: What would you like to do with it?

C: What do you call this?

M: A bowl.

C: What do you do with a bowl? (*Continues to chop at sand with spoon. Spills some sand on skirt and brushes it off.*) What do you think I'm doing? I think I'm chopping.

M: Oh, is that what you're doing? What Mommy makes?

C: (*Takes small doll from dollhouse. Picks up small bottle from bench and feeds doll. Has mother remove nipple from bottle and then continues to feed doll. Walks around room holding doll and bottle.*) She's drinking a lot of water already. There's no more water, baby. Hurry! Drink it.

T: She's got to drink it in a hurry or she doesn't get any more.

C: Drink the water, baby, or you won't get any more. If she doesn't drink it up, there won't be any more.

T: Nothing else for her if she doesn't do as she's told.

C: You gotta drink this, baby. Drink up. Drink up, baby. Quick! You gotta drink up, baby. (*Stands in front of mother and feeds doll.*) I don't think she's got enough water. There. You know you gotta drink the water. Drink it. She's drinking. Oh, baby! (*Laughs.*) Drink some more. (*Puts doll and bottle on bench. Picks up large bottle and looks at mother.*) Mama, I gotta have a big baby. (*Picks up a balloon and holds it.*) You know who's gonna get this one? Mama. Mama, take this one. (*Hands mother the balloon. Pours water from large bottle into washing machine. Places bottle and washer on floor and picks up doll and small bottle. Hands bottle to mother.*) You feed her.

M: All right.

C: (*Holds doll while mother feeds it.*) Look, Mama. My sleeve got wet.

M: It'll dry, honey.

C: It's wet.

M: It'll dry, dear.

C: Push my sleeve up, Mommy. (*Hands doll to mother.*) Mommy, take the baby.

M: You want me to take it?

C: Take it off. Take the diaper off.

T: You tell Mommy just what to do.

C: Gotta wash it now. (*Carries diaper to washing machine. Stuffs it into machine. Takes diaper out of machine and dips it into dish with sand. Stuffs it back into washing machine again. Takes it out again and rubs it in sand. Puts it into machine but immediately takes it out and puts it back into dish of sand. Pounds at diaper with small hammer. Rubs it in sand again. Looks at mother briefly. Continues to handle sand and diaper.*)

T: I guess that'll be all for today, Kathy. We've got to leave now.

C: (*Looks at T and brushes sand from her hands.*) Mommy, read me one of those magazines.

M: You mean the ones upstairs?

C: Yes, those. (*Walks out of room with mother and T.*)

Discussion

In this session, Kathy continued her play in the sand, talking incessantly while playing. She chatters constantly and seemingly diverts her mother while she messes in the sand.

Kathy's attention span in her play is now much longer and more concentrated. She still becomes upset when she gets sand on herself and wipes hard at the sand until it is all removed. She feeds the baby doll, repeating frequently that the baby *has* to eat. She reenacts the compulsive washing of the diaper, scrubbing it over and over again.

November 16. Interview with Father

T: Well, how has everything been going?

F: Look. First time in my life I have started to smoke. This thing has really got me. I have a few reasons why I believe Kathy is anxious and indefinite, saying one thing and then two seconds later saying, "I want this thing." This is probably caused by me for a couple of reasons. For one thing, the incident I told you about picking her up and saying, "We're going to bed." That was when she started having these fears at night. She pushed on my chest and didn't want me to take her. It may have been she didn't want to go up. I pushed her down. I should have treated her more gently. I shouldn't have pushed her so hard.

My wife tells me she mentions me every day. I believe her. Another incident—when I used to go in the room when she cried to herself it was as if she was holding something back. I would go in and ask her what was wrong. She wouldn't answer—probably she was afraid. It was probably the tone of voice that I used, as if to say, "What the hell are you crying for when it's time to sleep?" When I picked her up and said, "Put your arms around me," she looked at me askance.

T: You felt that she was drawing away from you.

F: I felt rejected by her. She was looking at me in a certain way as though I had done something terrible. Another thing—she would ask me for something, and I would say "no" in a way that she couldn't take. Now I say "no" in a different way—easier and more matter of fact.

I was going to drop this appointment, but I felt I had to come and face this. I have always had that feeling that I must face myself. Did my wife mention to you something about the time when she was close to me for several months and the relation was fine and cozy? One night she woke up crying, and from that time on, her actions became worse.

T: Something happened that night to frighten her.

F: We talked it over, and we tried to think over what happened. My wife says I spoke in a sharp tone, but I really can't remember that I did.

T: You can't remember exactly what happened then.

F: That's one trouble about me. I don't want perfection, and yet when it isn't there, I want it. Whether it comes out of my back life or not, I'm not sure.

T: There's something about you that insists on perfection and yet fights against it.

F: I will explain it the way I think. When I was twelve, I came to live with my real father and his second wife. My father had two children—my sister and me—in his former marriage and two children by this marriage, and she had one child by her former marriage. There were a lot of different personalities. It was obvious that I was the black sheep of the family. I was called a dumbbell practically every other day. My father never put his foot down.

T: They made you feel unimportant and stupid.

F: You see, my brother Jim, who is now a dancer, was given lessons on the piano, and my sister, too, but they figured I was too dumb to take lessons. Yet I like music. I can sit down at the piano and can play by ear, and I have always loved it. I was never given a chance to go to college. When the crash came, I had to help out and give everything I earned home. Years later I felt very resentful at that. Down deep I have no hatred for anyone. Yet I know I don't love anyone from my family.

T: In spite of what's happened, down deep you can't hate anyone.

F: I couldn't tolerate it within myself that I would really deeply hate anyone.

T: You would consider that a weakness.

F: I don't know. I don't want to be hated. Since I have been married, I have known real love. When I lived with my parents, I never thought I would marry a girl who would consider me good enough to love her. I felt no woman would ever want me and say "I love you."

T: You didn't feel good enough.

F: Yes. I never brought friends up to the house. I never had the feeling that they would be wanted. This is something that's passing, and yet it all comes back. One time I was going to meet a girl. I thought she was good-looking. My stepmother saw her and made a remark about the girl not being good-looking at all, and that struck me that no good-looking girl would ever go with me. That's the way I took her remark. That's what I thought she meant. Now I can see her ignorance made her that way.

T: You understand what made her say things like that.

F: It was a very poor relation between me and my father and stepmother. My wife is the only person who ever made me feel wanted. She loved me for what I was. Now she tells me she sees real goodness in me. Anything that I could do good in, I felt the fullest enjoyment from, and I felt good when someone outside told me I could do good. That's why sometimes I act childish when someone says I do well. I revel in it.

T: You really are affected by other people's praises.

F: That's how my wife looks at me. She respects me. It has been wonderful for me.

T: She has really helped you to gain faith in yourself.

F: (*Pause.*) It is just a few days, I have been thinking, that Kathy will get over her fears and she will come back to a normal relationship with me. Now I know it will take time. This fear of hers is great, but I know she can't have it all her life. The only thing is I want her to be normal, but I can't say I want Kathy to be a normal child at any price.

T: I see.

F: I don't want to lose her affection, and yet I want her to lose her fears. I feel that if she returns to normalcy, then our former relationship will return. If she gets over the fears, then it will come back. It is just the idea of me being very patient with the child and facing the situation with kindness and love.

T: You can look at her fears and her with more love than you have before.

F: Maybe that's right. (*Pause.*) My wife told me I shouldn't try to make Kathy be happy all the time, and I think it's just an excellent suggestion. Instead of saying, "Don't do that," to her in a harsh tone, I could try to explain that I have something to do and that I will play with her later.

T: You could accept her feelings and at the same time set a limit.

F: You brought up another point there. Here's something—I don't do it anymore, but a couple of times I used to say, "If you don't get in here by the time I count three, I will come and get you." Then one time she was fooling around in the sink way past her bedtime, and she said, "Aren't you going to count to three, Daddy?" She had that look in her eye, and it really made me feel bad, so I said, "Go ahead, honey. Finish what you're doing." Then

I said, "I won't count anymore." I didn't want her to reject me. I had the feeling that she wanted to be bossed or spanked. I felt she wanted to be spanked. I felt she wanted me to say, "You really can't do that," and that she wanted me to stick to it.

T: She felt more secure when you set some limits.

F: That's another way of putting what I am trying to say. I see what you're trying to say. Now when we go up there at night, she decides she wants to clean the sink out. I figure this way lately: "Anyway, it wouldn't hurt."

T: As long as it doesn't hurt anybody, you might as well let her do it.

F: I now have it clear in my mind. I am just going to be myself. I have been afraid before that she would reject me, but now I know I must do what I feel is right. I now realize I can make a decision and stand by it. This has helped a lot. I feel right. This is what I can do. I won't be back unless I get into a turmoil again, but I don't feel that I will.

November 22. Play Session with Kathy and Mother

C: (*Runs into room. Picks up a hand puppet and examines it.*) What is that?

M: It's a puppet.

C: A puppet?

M: Mm-hm.

C: What do you do to puppets? What do you do with them? (*Handles puppet.*) Mommy, look. It's just like on television.

M: Mm-hm.

C: (*Hands puppet to mother and picks up a rubber knife.*) What do you do with this? How do you cut?

M: You know how.

C: What do you do with the knifes?

M: You cut with them.

C: How you cut? (*Extends knife to mother.*) Here. Reach over. Here.

M: Are you too lazy to walk over here?

C: Here, reach. Let's see how you cut.

M: You show me how to cut.

C: (*Cuts at table with knife.*) See how you cut? That's how you cut this. Hold it nice and straight and you cut. (*Throws knife on the floor.*) Get this little shovel and dig in the dirt. There's a whole bunch of dirt. This goes in the yellow truck. (*Puts a spoonful of sand from sandbox into truck. Handles sand.*) A duty. I gotta make, Mommy.

M: All right.

C: (*Goes out to bathroom with mother. Walks back into room and picks up the steam shovel.*) Here's a steam shovel. Mommy's gonna get this. (*Hands a puppet to T.*) And here's a bunny for you. You can have that. (*Continues to play in sand.*)

———·———

C: (*Picks up gun and handles it. Aims at mother.*) Bang, bang, bang. (*Moves to sandbox and looks at T.*) I burned myself on popcorn. Where did you burn yourself, Mommy?

M: On the oven.

C: She burned herself on the oven.

T: And you hurt yourself on the popcorn popper.

C: Yes, I burned myself on the popcorn popper. I love popcorn. (*Dances around a little near the sandbox.*) You know, I don't like my Aunty Ann.

T: You don't.

C: No. What don't I like where my Aunty Ann lives?

M: Oh, you mean the sign?

C: Yes, the sign.

T: Is that why you don't like Aunty Ann? Because she has a sign near her house?

C: She lives by it, but she doesn't live way far from it.

T: Mm-hm.

C: (*Digs in the sandbox with the steam shovel. Carries some sand to truck.*) You're the stupid mother that I ever saw in my life.

M: You think I'm stupid, honey?

C: You're the most stupid old mother that I ever saw in my life.
You're the stupid old mother that I ever saw. (*Handles steam
shovel.*) Why is this dirty?

M: Well, you were using it in the sand.

C: Take this off.

M: You can take it off.

T: You want Mommy to do it.

C: I want her to do it.

T: You want her to do it but she wants you to do it.

C: I always like to make her work. (*Brushes sand from hands while
walking around room. Picks up small nursing bottle.*) Where's the
baby? (*Picks up small doll.*) I'm gonna wash the diaper in the
washing machine so the diaper will be nice and clean. I want to
soak it in the bottle. (*Picks up large nursing bottle.*) I need the big
bottle. And I'll soak it right in the big bottle. Take the pin off.
(*Watches T as he unpins doll's diaper. Takes the diaper off and
lets the doll fall to the floor.*) Drop goes the baby. Soak. (*Dips doll's
diaper into large bottle of water.*)

T: You want to stick it right down in there.

C: (*Continues to stuff diaper into bottle.*) Mommy, you hold this. You
hold it. I'm tired of holding it.

M: You're tired?

C: (*Soaks diaper in bottle while mother holds the bottle.*)

T: You're poking it right down in there.

C: Oh! What you call it when I couldn't go on the merry-go-round?
Polio?

M: Mm-hm.

C: Polio. Polio's a very bad cold. Polio's a *very* bad cold! Isn't polio
a very bad cold?

M: Mm-hm.

C: Polio. (*Still soaking diaper in bottle.*) Once when I took my boots
off, my hands got all full of dirt.

T: You got your hands pretty dirty, hm?

C: Uh-huh. Then once I got my hands all full of mud.

T: You didn't like that, did you?

C: No. (*Removes diaper from bottle and squeezes water from it on the floor. Dips it into bottle again.*) And now I'll let it soak.

T: You're soaking it real good.

C: Now I'll take it. (*Takes bottle from mother and places it on table. Takes diaper out of bottle. Stamps on the floor.*) Voulez vous, Mom. Voulez vous. That's what Daddy says.

M: In French?

C: Yeah. In French. What does he say in French? (*Jumps up and down while holding diaper.*)

M: Voulez vous.

C: Voulez vous.

T: You like to talk about your daddy's French, hm?

C: When Daddy takes off his shoes and socks, he goes like this. Like this. Like that. (*Shows T how her father acts without shoes on.*)

M: Is that how Daddy keeps his feet when he hasn't got any shoes on?

C: Uh-huh.

T: You like to do what your daddy does?

C: When he hasn't got his shoes on, then he goes like this.

T: Is that what you like to do?

C: Uh-huh. When my feet are cold. (*Soaks diaper again.*) Stuck that in and let it soak. (*Drops sand in bottle.*) This has gotta go in dirty water.

T: Mm-hm.

C: (*Drops bells into bottle.*) It goes right in the water. Put your jingle in. I've gotta make a duty.

M: All right. Come on.

C: (*Walks out to bathroom with mother. Walks back into room and smiles at T.*) I drowned myself. I drowned myself.

T: You drowned yourself, hm?

C: (*Picks up doll and pushes its head into dish of water.*) Gonna stick her head in.

T: You're going to put her right into the water.

C: She has to make. She has to make sissy. (*Picks up a rubber cord and pushes it at doll's genital area.*) She has to make. O.K., come on. Make sissy. Come on, make duty. Now you have to make. (*Pushes cord in water on floor. Picks up dish and spills water on floor near puppet. Places dish and doll on chair and sticks cord into large nursing bottle.*) Take the diaper out. It smells. It's gonna be all smelly. (*Hands bottle with diaper in it to mother.*) Here's the diaper. Will you get the diaper out? Will you get the diaper out?

T: You want Mommy to get the diaper out, hm?

C: Get the diaper out. (*Takes bottle back from mother and tries to shake the diaper out of it.*) Here it is. Now.

T: Well, Kathy, that's all the time we have left today. Our time is just up.

C: Mommy, will you read me a magazine? (*Looks at T.*) Bye.

T: Good-bye, Kathy.

C: Bye. (*Walks out of room with mother.*)

Discussion

Kathy repeatedly questions her mother. She is generally anxious in her play. As the session unfolds, hostility toward her mother becomes direct. She picks up a toy gun, aims it at her mother, and shouts, "Bang, bang, bang." Then she expresses feelings of anger against an aunt. Later she looks at her mother and says, "You're the stupid mother that I ever saw in my life. . . . You're the most stupid old mother that I ever saw. . . ." Kathy asks her mother to remove sand from a shovel and explains, "I always like to make her work."

The diaper-washing play begins again. Her cleanliness anxiety is further explored as she scrubs the diaper and indicates to the therapist that she does not like to see dirt on herself.

Kathy reveals positive feelings toward her father, repeating what he says and mimicking his behavior.

Toward the end of the session the compulsive behavior reappears. Kathy picks up the baby doll and shouts, "She has to make. She has to make sissy. She has to make. O.K., come on. Make sissy. Come on, make duty. Now you have to make." This episode may reflect the pressures Kathy has faced in the cleanliness and toileting demands at home.

November 22. Telephone Conversation with Father

F: I wanted to talk to you. Before I came to see you, my stomach would turn over. I couldn't eat and I couldn't sleep. I didn't know how to act. I would be afraid to do anything for fear it would be the wrong thing. All I thought about was that. Now I've been eating and sleeping more regularly. I've been working without being worried.

I talked to my wife about what you told me. Will you explain to her in your own way? That was the whole key as far as discipline is concerned. I hardly ever gave her any discipline at all, yet she seemed like she wanted to be told she couldn't do certain things. I tried to explain it to my wife but found it difficult. I understood it in terms of myself, but it was difficult to explain it to her so she could see it in terms of herself.

When it was time to eat, Kathy would pick up one plate and another and another. She was never satisfied. A couple of nights ago I said, "Kathy, you will eat from that plate. You don't have to eat if you don't want to." Two seconds later she ate the whole plate and talked and laughed throughout the whole meal. She seemed perfectly satisfied. And furthermore, I think that no matter how I treated her she would always love me anyway. No matter how much discipline I used, within limits, she would always love me and I would love her.

One more point I noticed. You have made me see things I haven't seen. I may have been too mixed up. Now I am not. Sometimes I've noticed during the day we're right in the room and she'll say, "Where are you?" I realized if I don't answer she goes right on in her play. I am not afraid any more. I feel good now. I don't worry about her at work. Now I am like I was before. I haven't changed myself. I am still myself. I'm happy about things now. Well, I won't take any more of your time. Thank you very much.

November 23. Interview with Mother

M: I don't know what happened, but she's just as changed as ever. After the last time I talked to you we let her sleep on the daybed, and then we ordered a Hollywood bed. That part has settled the sleeping problem, but something might still crop up.

   Today she wanted to play with her finger paints, and I said, "We have to go downtown first," and she said, "O.K.," right away, whereas before when she wanted to do something, she was determined to do it right at that moment.

   There is something I wanted to tell you that I forgot. Remember when I told you she didn't want to have anything to do with her daddy? She was just clinging to me. I know she loves me, and it doesn't bother me. In order to get her to make up to him, I kept saying, "Go to Daddy." I kept saying "Go to Daddy," and the way I said it may have made her feel I didn't want her. I have shown her in every way I could that I love her.

T: She may have felt you didn't want her, even though you have shown her that you loved her.

M: Maybe she felt that I rejected her, too, because she wouldn't go to Daddy and then, see, I would say, "Let Daddy dress you." I was trying to get her out of it by pushing her. When she was mad at her father, I think she should have been allowed to get it out of her system.

T: She should have been allowed to bring out her feelings, no matter how they affected your husband.

M: Yes. Something else I wanted to ask you. I don't know how to act when I am in the playroom. I try to act the way you do. I am a little strained. I felt silly. If I see she's having difficulty, then I help her. If I am myself, it won't change anything. She doesn't talk about it. She says, "Are we going to see Mr. C? Are we going to play today?"

T: She looks forward to coming here.

M: Let's see if there was something else. She's not afraid of any signs any more. She'll say, "I don't like the arm." Today I went right by it and explained to her, and she stared right at it, and she said, "Oh, look there, Mommy. You went right by that sign," and she laughed about it. She had no connection with her fears. I have not noticed any fears at all. She's not as rebellious as she was. She doesn't like to go to bed yet, but it's not because she's afraid. She just likes to stay up with us. We got hold of you right away when the fears first started. They had only gone for a short time. I hope it is disappearing forever now. I feel very much better about the whole thing, because she is improving. You wouldn't ever know what we went through. She used to be terrified. There are no more eyes now, no more fear of eyes.

I meant to tell you—when she plays in the yard she'll sit down and sit at the sand and play for a long time like she would in the playroom. This has all started recently. She does that all the time. Not seeing those books for three months, the other day she read by heart every one of them. So she must have a pretty good memory to be able to do that.

(*Pause.*) I guess there won't be any need for me to come down anymore, but if you decide that there are other things that come up later, in terms of Kathy's play in the playroom, then I'll make an appointment with you.

December 5. Play Session with Kathy and Mother

C: (*Runs into the room. Walks near T and then goes to pile of furniture.*) Where's the diaper? Take the diaper off this baby. Mommy! (*Runs out to hall to find mother.*)

M: I'm coming in.

T: You like to have Mommy right near you.

C: Here. Here's a mask.

T: You want me to have a mask. O.K.

C: No. Mommy wear a mask. (*Takes mask from T and gives it to mother.*) I'm gonna make supper. (*Sits near table. Stands up to move chair closer, then sits down again. Picks up dish and walks to mother.*) Well, I don't need the chopping bowl. Gonna make chopped liver. I—Mommy—Mommy, do you make chopped liver? I like chopped liver.

M: Mm-hm.

C: (*Picks up sieve, fills it with sand, then empties it into dish.*) Gonna have chopped liver. You can make it a different kind. See this, Mommy? That's to make chopped liver with. Pick it up and put it in here. Now I'm gonna chop it. (*Holds dish with sand in lap and chops at sand with shovel.*) This is a neat chopping bowl. Baby's gonna have some of that, too. I gotta chop it.

T: You want the baby to have the chopped liver, hm?

C: Oh! There we go. (*Spills some sand on her socks.*) On my sock. I did it on purpose.

T: You mean you put it on you on purpose, hm?

C: These are my good socks. I wear them every day.

T: And you didn't care. You did it anyway.

C: Here we go again. (*Spills sand on her dress and brushes it off. Stirs sand with shovel.*) Daddy says, "I don't love you."

T: Daddy says that he doesn't love you, hm?

C: No. I say I don't love Daddy.

T: Oh, you don't love Daddy.

C: No. Daddy said if I don't eat dinner, then he doesn't bring me any surprises. He says, "If you won't eat, then I won't bring you any surprises."

T: Oh, your daddy tells you you've got to eat, hm?

C: Uh-huh.

T: And you don't like that, is that it?

C: I'll play with chopped liver. Once Donna threw sand once. In my eyes once.

T: She threw sand right in your eyes.

C: And Mommy had to wash it out. (*Starts to chop sand with shovel again.*) It's dirty over here. Do you know that, Mommy?

T: You don't like the dirt, hm?

C: No. Just the sand. I don't like how soft and sticky it gets. It always makes me sad.

T: That makes you sad, hm?

C: Uh-huh. It's always hard to make. You chop and you chop and you go like this. (*Continues to chop sand in dish.*) And I'll chop, chop, chop. Chopping, chopping, chop, chop, chop. Gonna make it. It's gonna be ready in just a couple minutes. Mommy's gonna have good chopped liver. (*Puts dish on table and brushes sand from her hands. Picks up rubber doll and feeds it with small bottle.*) The baby has to drink water 'cause she's thirsty. She'll have to stay right here. Like this she can drink.

T: Mm-hm.

C: She's gotta drink a lot of water. She doesn't drink the water.

T: She doesn't?

C: Gonna drink all the water up. Chopped liver is ready, baby. She likes chopped liver. If I make chopped liver for her, she always eats it up. She always likes it. She always likes chopped liver.

T: She really likes to eat that.

C: Mm-hm. (*Continues to spoon sand into doll's mouth.*) She's got a surprise coming. You know what it is? A sucker. She's getting a sucker and chocolate. And bubble gum.

T: Three surprises, and all for her.

C: Mm-hm. I never get that many surprises.

T: You never get that many surprises, hm?

C: No. She likes that chopped liver. Eat, baby. Eat, baby. Eat, baby. She says she likes chopped liver. She doesn't waste it. She keeps it all in her mouth. Eat, baby. Eat, baby. She says, "Yes, I will eat."

T: She eats when you tell her to.

C: (*Feeds doll with small bottle.*) Swallow, baby. Good. She likes— she can't swallow it.

T: No?

C: No, she can't. Oh, good thing she doesn't like chopped liver.

T: Why?

C: 'Cause she doesn't. (*Feeds doll more sand.*) Also, she can't have no more surprises. (*Stamps her foot on the floor.*)

T: No more surprises for her, hm?

C: No.

T: Because she won't eat her chopped liver.

C: No. She doesn't like it.

T: She must feel bad.

C: But she's gonna eat a little bit. (*Feeds doll a small spoonful of sand.*) Come on, baby. Take a little bit. You always have to eat it all. She's gotta eat that or no chocolate. (*Leaves doll on the table. Picks up a sheet of paper and cuts it into small pieces. Dips piece of paper into large bottle of water and then places wet paper on car.*) Put that on the back of the car. There. Now. (*Wets more pieces of paper.*) Now. Put some right on this truck. (*Pastes wet pieces of paper on cars and trucks for the remainder of the hour.*)

Discussion

In the December 5 session, Kathy spills sand on herself and is not at all perturbed. She exclaims, "Daddy said if I don't eat dinner, then he doesn't bring me any surprises." Kathy has frequently shown, in her play, strong feelings against forced feedings. In this session, feelings connected with food are primarily positive. The baby is not forced to eat. The baby enjoys eating. "She always likes chopped liver." The feeding scene is reenacted over and over again. Kathy is ambivalent at points. The baby enjoys food yet does not always like to eat. Kathy explores and re-explores negative and ambivalent feelings with reference to food and as she does her spontaneity is heightened and she brings more joy into her play.

December 5. Telephone Conversation with Father

F: I just got an idea that may be the cause of it all. Probably not, but my wife thinks so. She thinks that Kathy has a fear that we will leave her. If we go on the street, she's afraid we're going to send her away. She thinks we'll leave her and she won't see us again. Now we're worried, though not as much as before. She talks more about her fears. Will she outgrow this? If you were to say "yes" and mean it, then I would never have any worries.

Last night she started to whimper. I said, "There's no reason to cry. I'm here, and I'll protect you. You don't have to cry," and she stopped crying. We'd been losing sleep. She'd wake up and cry and whimper, but this time when we went in, she told us what she was afraid of. Personally, I don't care. We'll just have to string along until she gets better. Kathy is no different from other children. All children have fears. She'll get over this.

December 13. Play Session with Kathy and Mother

C: (*Runs into the room.*)

T: Well, everything is all set for you, Kathy.

C: O.K. (*Carries chair to table and sits down.*) Mommy.

M: Hmm?

C: Mommy, my feet are frozen.

M: Well, they'll warm up.

C: This is a little balloon. Here. That little balloon for you. (*Hands T a small balloon.*) And a big balloon for Mommy. Here's a big one for you.

M: Thank you.

C: And you've got a little balloon. (*Picks up puppets from floor and hands them to T.*) Here's a puppet for you. Two puppets.

T: You want me to have these.

C: There's a toad chasing me, Mom. (*Runs to mother and hugs her. Looks at T.*)

T: A toad is chasing you?

C: Yes.

T: Are you afraid he's going to get you?

C: Yeah. There's a bad toad catching me, Mom.

T: You really are afraid of that toad.

C: You're gonna get a puppet. A different kind of puppet. Here's your puppet. A pretty puppet. Here's another puppet. You got two puppets, too. (*Hands two animal puppets to mother.*)

M: Thank you.

C: (*Picks up large nursing bottle.*) I don't drink water out of this.

T: You don't?

C: No. Babies drink out of that. I don't have to wash the diapers every time.

T: You don't have to wash them every time?

C: No. (*Holds doll and sits on chair.*) Every time she wears them, every time they get dirty. (*Dips rubber cord into bottle and pushes cord into doll's mouth.*) You like water? She says "I like water very much." That's what she likes. She says "I want some water."

T: And you let her have the water.

C: No surprises for her.

T: You didn't give her any surprises, hm?

C: No. Because she didn't like water. She wants some milk now. Daddy teases me.

T: He really teases you. And do you like that?

C: Well, yes, I like that. When I chew the gum he laughs at me.

T: He laughs at you.

C: Mm-hm. (*Picks up small bottle.*) Baby, baby. Wash your hair. You need a shampoo. (*Wants mother to remove the nipple from bottle.*) Get this off. I gotta wash her hair.

M: You can do it yourself.

C: I can't.

M: Try it.

C: No. (*Mother removes nipple and C empties water from small bottle into dish. Empties water from dish into sandbox. Puts sand in dish with steam shovel.*) I'll wash your hair. (*Crouches by sandbox.*) I'm getting dirty today. (*Pause.*) Mommy has skim milk, but I don't like skim milk. Mommy's on a diet. I'm not on a diet. (*Mother laughs.*)

T: Oh.

C: (*Fills dish with sand and carries it to table. Picks up doll and holds it over dish.*) She has to make sissy. She has to make sissy. (*Wants T to unpin doll's diaper.*) Unpin it. Unpin it.

T: There we are.

C: (*Holds diaperless doll over dish.*) Make. She doesn't have to.

T: She doesn't have to make sissy?

C: (*Hands diaper to mother.*) Here. You're gonna hold the diaper.

M: O.K.

C: (*Picks up some sand and rubs it all over doll's head.*) I'll just wash this right off. (*Stands up and brushes sand from dress vigorously.*) My good dress!

T: It's all sandy and you don't like that.

C: No. It's the best dress I ever bought.

T: Oh.

C: My hands are dirty. (*Picks up rubber knife. Pokes at sand in hand with knife.*) This is a big knife. It's sharp. It's sharp. You know that, Mom?

M: Mm-hm.

C: (*Pokes blade of knife on palm of her hand.*) This knife is really sharp. Sharp, sharp, sharp. (*Puts knife back on table and picks up shovel. Chops at sand in dish.*) Chop, chop. (*Continues to chop at sand.*) Baby, your chopped liver is ready. Do you like chopped liver? What do you want to eat it with? This? No, you gotta eat it out of this.

T: She has to eat it out of what you tell her to.

C: A spoon. (*Feeds doll sand from spoon.*) If she wants some chopped liver, she says, "I want some chopped liver." And I made it for her. Just for her. (*Looks at mother, then at T.*) You remember when Donna used to throw sand in my eyes? And I used to throw sand back in her eyes.

T: She used to do that, hm?

C: Yeah. And I used to throw sand in her eyes. And I didn't like that, and Mommy had to wash the sand out. Poor baby. She's thirsty. Well, baby, you're gonna get something. Oh, she likes it. (*Puts doll on table and picks up dish with sand. Walks to mother.*) Now, Mommy. Hold my gum. (*Gives mother her chewing gum.*)

M: O.K., dear.

C: (*Looks at T.*) Can you put it in your mouth, like that? How you put it in your mouth?

T: You show me.

C: O.K. Like this. (*Puts some sand on paddle and tastes it. Spits sand out on floor.*)

T: It doesn't taste good, does it?

C: I don't like it. (*Stirs paddle around in dish. Tastes sand again and makes a face.*) You know, sand is sour. Is sand sour?

T: What do you think?

C: It's not sour but it tastes sour to me. (*Tastes more sand and spits it back into dish.*) It's not sour but it tastes sour. (*Wipes mouth with diaper.*) The diaper's dirty anyway. It's like a towel. (*Tastes more sand and spits it out. Eats and spits sand again.*) Pooh! That's what I used to say when I had sand in my house.

M: Honey, do you want your gum?

C: (*Dances up and down in front of mother.*) I don't want it. I don't want to chew it. Throw it away! Throw the gum away. In the street. Throw it away in the street! (*Puts dish on table and picks up a balloon. Runs back and forth across room.*) I can run fast.

T: You can?

C: Mm-hm. Let me show you. Let me show you how fast. Let me show you. (*Runs across room.*) I can run real fast. Here comes a wolf! (*Runs to mother and waves balloon in the air.*)

T: You can run real fast when the wolf is coming, can't you?

C: Yes. Right against the wall.

T: You really hit the wolf, hm?

C: Yes. He wants to take the balloon away. He wants to throw it away in the street. (*Jumps up and down and balloon falls into sandbox. Picks it up and leans against mother.*) There's a wolf!

T: You're really afraid of the wolf, hm?

C: Yes. I am. (*Waves balloon around.*) I'm afraid of the toads.

T: You're afraid of the toads?

C: Mm-hm. (*Tosses balloon aside and picks up bells. Jingles them and jumps up and down. Places bells on chair and turns to mother.*) I wanta go now. Now!

T: You want to leave now, Kathy?

C: Yes.

T: You still have a minute or so left if you want to stay. You can go if you want to, though. It's up to you.

C: I wanta stay.

T: You want to stay for two more minutes?

C: Uh-huh. (*Picks up bells again.*)

T: O.K.

C: And now, where's a knife? Where's a knife? I can't find the knife.

T: You need the knife, hm?

C: The knife. Here's a knife, but I don't want to use that knife. (*Picks up a rubber knife but puts it back on table*.) Everything I pick up, I put down. (*Holds balls and runs to mother*.) Here comes the wolf! The bad wolf! Let me sit in your lap.

T: The real bad wolf is coming and you're afraid.

C: Yes. Let me sit in your lap. (*Settles herself in mother's lap*.) Now. Now he can't hurt me.

T: When you're on Mommy's lap, the wolf can't hurt you?

C: No, he can't hurt me. (*Sits in mother's lap and jingles the bells*.)

T: Kathy, our time is up for today.

C: (*Hands T the bells and helps mother put down the toys she has been holding*.) I'll be back. (*Walks out of the room with mother and T*.)

Discussion

In the playroom, Kathy enacts fears that she has expressed at home with her parents. She runs to her mother, claiming that "There's a wolf!" and that "the bad toad" is after her. She stays near her mother for a while, then starts playing again. She expresses positive feelings toward her father again, imitating his behavior with enjoyment. She indicates a willingness to face her anxiety about cleanliness, exclaiming, "I'm getting dirty today."

Kathy plays out a forced toileting scene, feeling less pressure. She plays freely in the sand for a prolonged time. Suddenly her fears return. She runs to her mother, claiming that a wolf is chasing her. Then, showing she is not so frightened anymore, she strikes back at an imaginary wolf. Near the end of the session she becomes frightened again and sits on her mother's lap.

December 14. Interview with Mother

M: I'll tell you what I learned. She said there was a wolf chasing her, trying to chase her out of the house. She would get hurt by a car and would go far, far away and wouldn't see Mommy and Daddy again. Or else she would get burned by a fire. Maybe we stressed that harm might come to her too much, if she wasn't careful. She keeps asking questions. Maybe she's afraid.

She used to wake up and cry. Now that we've tried to understand her feelings, she wakes up and tells us about her fears. She talks to us. She tells us. She used to draw away from my husband, but now she doesn't. She'll hold onto either one of us.

She saw a toad on T.V. and said this toad was trying to chase her out of the house. All of a sudden she has started this clinging business. The wolf I know she got from her books. I remember once I said to her, "Kathy, if you don't behave, I'll call it off." She misunderstood and said, "Why are you going to call the wolf?" I think I have it all figured out, and then when I think about it, I get all mixed up. She talks about the wolf trying to chase her. She lays there in bed until nine-thirty. This goes on every night. She thinks and thinks and thinks before she goes to bed.

I would like to know what brought it back in the first place. She was just fine. She used to sing in bed. Now she wakes up continually. For four nights I had to sleep with her, but she never slept. She couldn't have slept more than five hours a night. We tried to give her confidence. We're befuddled. When she's well rested when she gets up she's better. She doesn't think too much, so she doesn't think of the fears. She's still afraid of the strong arm. My husband would say, "Honey, don't be afraid of anything. We won't let anything hurt you." He'd say, "You see this arm, honey? I can protect you with it." He'd show her it, and now she's afraid of that arm. At home he goes around wearing polo shirts, and he'd show her his strong arm. It seems to be the logical connection.

T: She's afraid of him, then.

M: Of course she's afraid of other things. She doesn't like the giraffe on the sign. Yesterday she said the bad eye was chasing her. Remember the bird on the telephone book? She said that the bird is in the room. What made her all right during that period? What made her go back? Before, we tried to reason with her. Now when she's afraid of something, I try to understand it. When she told me about the car hurting her and our going away, I said, "If you get hurt by a car of if you get burned or get hurt, we'll always be there." I tried to show her we'd be there with her.

I know she loves her daddy. When he comes home, she's so excited she can hardly wait for him to come home.

December 20. Play Session with Kathy and Mother

C: (*Hands T two puppets.*) Here. You're gonna have those two puppets.

T: You want me to have these two, hm?

C: Mommy's gonna get the other puppets. Here, Mommy. (*Hands mother animal puppets.*) Don't you mind getting those two puppets, Mommy?

M: No, honey. I don't mind.

C: (*Walks back and forth across room.*) You know what? I got something to tell you. You know what the flub-a-dub wanted?

T: What did the flub-a-dub want?

C: He says, "I want a present." The flub-a-dub says, "I want some spaghetti and meatballs." (*Jumps up and down and laughs.*) That's so funny.

T: You like to tell funny things, don't you?

C: Yeah. (*Laughs again.*) Isn't that funny? (*Picks up a boat and crouches by sandbox. Fills boat with sand.*) Now I'm gonna make some sand. I'm gonna smooth the sand out. (*Hands boat to mother.*) Here, Mom. Here's some for you. You're gonna get this. With a little shovel. Here, eat it. (*Walks around room.*) A wolf's chasing me!

T: Is a wolf chasing you, Kathy?

C: A wolf's catching me.

T: The big bad wolf. And are you afraid?

C: No. I'm not afraid. I'm not afraid of the wolf. (*Picks up a paddle from the table.*) This is what I was looking for. (*Tastes some sand from boat with paddle.*) I'm eating my supper. I'm gonna eat my supper now. (*Sits down on chair and tastes more sand.*) I'm gonna give Daddy dinner. He's gonna eat out of the shovel. And I'll eat out of it.

T: You and Daddy will eat out of the same shovel.

C: No, he's gonna eat the shovel.

T: Oh, he's going to eat the shovel?

C: Mm-hm. Where's the shovel? No shovels. So Daddy will have to go to bed. (*Tastes sand and makes a face.*) He'll have to go to bed with no surprises.

T: No surprise for Daddy, hm?

C: No. 'Cause he wasn't good.

T: He wasn't good to you, hm?

C: No.

T: So to bed with him without anything.

C: Yeah. And he didn't want to go to bed.

T: He didn't?

C: No.

T: He didn't like not having surprises, hm?

C: No. He doesn't like not having surprises. (*Handles paddle and tastes sand. Looks at T.*) I forgot to give Daddy a drink of water, and he was thirsty.

T: He was thirsty, and you forgot to give Daddy a drink of water, hm?

C: But I'm not gonna.

T: You're not going to do it?

C: No.

T: He'll have to go without any.

C: Uh-huh. I didn't kiss him good night.

T: Didn't you?

C: Uh-huh. (*Takes puppets from mother, together with two on floor, and hands them to T.*) And you're gonna get puppets. Here's puppets for you.

T: All the puppets are going to me.

C: 'Cause Mommy doesn't want any puppets.

T: She doesn't, hm?

C: (*Looks at mother.*) She has to stay up. And a surprise for Mommy.

T: Oh, you're going to give Mommy a surprise, are you?

C: Mm-hm. (*Tastes more sand and spits it out on the floor.*) Then a drink of water, and then she's going upstairs to bed. And tonight is my dinner, and I'm going right up. And no surprise.

T: No surprise for you either.

C: No, 'cause I don't want surprises.

T: You don't even like them.

C: Daddy always brings me surprises.

T: He does?

C: Mmmm.

T: And are you happy about that?

C: (*Sighs heavily. Tastes sand, then spits it on the floor.*) Pooh!

T: It doesn't taste so good.

C: (*Stamps foot on the floor.*) Stamp, stamp. (*Hands mother the rubber cord.*) That silly old thing! This silly old thing that I ever saw! (*Hands mother the large doll.*) Mommy's gonna get all the presents.

T: They're all for Mommy.

C: And you're gonna get—here's a present for you. (*Hands T a small doll figure.*) You're gonna get all the presents. (*Hands T another small male doll.*) And Mommy's gonna get a girl. (*Hands mother a female doll.*)

M: Thank you, honey.

C: You're gonna get all the presents. Some more presents. You're gonna get all of 'em. (*Gives mother another small doll.*) Here's another present. (*Picks up dish and moves to sandbox. Fills dish with sand.*) Now I'll fix some chopped liver.

T: More chopped liver to chop, chop, chop.

C: (*Fills dish with more sand.*) Now get some more. And have another big bite. And still another big bite.

T: It goes on and on and on.

C: Yeah. It goes on and on and on. Gonna chop. (*Stamps foot on floor a few times.*) Stinky! Stinky! Stinky! (*Picks up doll. Sits on chair and pushes some sand into doll's mouth.*) What do you want? A drink of water? Here we go again! (*Replaces doll on table and walks back and forth across room.*)

T: All she asks for is more water and causes a lot of trouble.

C: Yeah. And she doesn't want no surprises 'cause she doesn't like surprises. (*Tugs at vise and pushes it back and forth.*) What a silly dumbbell I am.

T: Are you a silly dumbbell?

C: Yeah, I'm so silly. (*Pours some sand from dish into small bathtub. Then spills sand on rug.*) There! Spill that all on the rug.

T: Just spill it all over. That's the way you feel, hm?

C: (*Tosses tub aside. Picks up pieces of doll furniture and tosses them aside.*) I'll squeeze that out, and squeeze that out. And squeeze that out and squeeze that out.

T: Squeeze them all out.

C: And turn the squeezes out. And squeeze that out.

T: You want everything to be squeezed out.

C: (*Picks up part of the toy record player.*) This is a victrola. Squeeze that out. Squeeze that out. (*Continues to toss furniture to one side.*) I wanta go now.

T: Are you finished, Kathy? You still have a few minutes. You can stay if you like. If you want to go, it's up to you.

C: I wanta stay.

T: You want to stay for a few more minutes?

C: Uh-huh.

T: All right. There're just about three more minutes.

C: (*Scrapes sand from table onto floor with paddle.*) I'm gonna spill this all on the floor. (*Stamps on the sand.*) Stamp! Stamp! (*Drops paddle on floor and runs across room.*) The wolf's here. I'm gonna run to my mommy.

T: Are you afraid the wolf is chasing you?

C: And he's not gonna get me. (*Picks up doll from mother's lap and kisses it. Holds it up in the air. Holds doll's legs around her neck.*) Upsy-daisy. Upsy-daisy. Upsy-daisy. Upsy-daisy. Upsy-daisy. Upsy-daisy. She likes to go up.

T: Well, Kathy, our time is just about up for today.

C: O.K. (*Throws doll on the floor.*) Let's go, Mom. Good-bye.

T: Good-bye, Kathy.

C: Good-bye.

Discussion

Again Kathy expresses her fears directly, running to her mother and claiming "the wolf" is chasing her. She shows anger toward her father, retaliating in kind to his methods. She refuses to give her daddy a glass of water or a good-night kiss. She decides to give her mother the surprises and "all the presents." She rationalizes her own position with, "I don't want any surprises," and resists the pressures, refusing to eat dinner, surprises or no surprises. This scene is played out repeatedly.

Kathy spills water on the rug without concern. She attempts to crush various pieces of toy furniture, throws sand on the floor, and stamps her feet. These expressions of generalized anger are followed by fear. She runs to her mother and screams that "the wolf" is chasing her. In a final gesture she throws the baby doll onto the floor and leaves.

December 22. Telephone Conversation with Father

F: Oh, brother! What a mess! I think I had better see you and tell you a few things. I don't know what to do or say. Have you got any ideas? She'll get up at eight in the morning. She's so tired. We put her to bed, and she will not sleep. She calls her mother. She cries something fierce. Last night she wasn't getting on my nerves like she used to, even though she was interrupting our sleep.

A couple of nights ago she was still talking. I said, "Kathy, get out of bed if you don't sleep." She refuses to sleep. She wakes up at twelve-thirty or one, and when she wakes up, she's fully awake. Maybe I am seeing more than is really there. When she yawns, it isn't a full yawn. It's a forced one, and it's a fight against sleep. Like last night she didn't sleep well. She won't sleep through the night. Sometimes I feel like saying, "Kathy, you go to sleep."

It makes me feel very, very bad to see her like that. I realize that it was bad to try to make her perfect. Well, I'll come in and see you next week.

December 27. Interview with Father

F: The day I called you, my inside was in a turmoil, and I guess it's because Kathy was worse that day and the day before. When she starts to relax, then it shows more, and I feel better.

T: When she gets worse, then it makes you feel worse.

F: I know it is wrong to think that way. She gets better and then she gets worse and then gets better again and worse again. But each time the better is stronger and the worse is weaker. I think at that moment things will start slacking.

T: It's an unsteady process.

F: Sometimes I think it will fade, and sometimes I don't. The little son of a gun—she's so hard to figure out. It's going away, and I know it will. I think at that moment it's going to get better, and then it gets worse. Then when it seems hopeless, it gets better again.

T: It's really a puzzling matter then, isn't it?

F: I'll tell you a couple more incidents. (*Pause.*) This morning Kathy woke up early, as she often does, and she got into bed with my wife. It so happens our bedroom faces a road, and as the cars go by, they throw a passing shadow, and that's her bugaboo—any kind of shadow. She put her head on the pillow and didn't want to see the shadow. I said, "Come downstairs, Kathy, and talk to me. I have to go to work." She looked on the front window at the door. She glanced at it several times. I said, "Honey, do you know what a shadow is?" There were some shadows on the front room floor, so I took my hand and made shadows and said, "See, honey, the shadow is my hand," and I said, "Now you put your hand like that." A little later she yelled, "Ma," and told her what she saw. When I left for work I sensed it made no difference with her. She was still afraid of the shadows.

Last night after supper she started going down the basement, and halfway down she came back and said, "The train was chasing me." My wife asked, "What would happen if the train caught you?" and she said, "It would make me dead," and I said, "Not while we're here." These things are funny with her. Her fears of the shadows—she laughs while talking about it, but I notice that she's dead serious.

Now I'm getting a little nervous. Maybe it's talking about all this that makes me that way. Another thing, let me tell you. I stay with her now. She feels more secure with me in the room on the daybed. Instead of trying to make her stay by herself, I stay with her. Last night I told her two stories.

You remember the first time I came to see you, I was in one mess. I didn't know what to do. It seems as if she's gotten a lot better. At least she talks about it and tells you what she's afraid of. I would say she has improved.

I know where I failed. I failed to realize that I always thought Kathy to be abnormal, for instance. She eternally wanted to sit on my lap and do what I do. I see other kids are the same way. I realize that it is normal for a child to show so much affection.

T: For a while you were afraid she showed too much love, but now you accept it as normal.

F: I felt she was just sitting on my lap too much, and now I'm beginning to realize that it is her search for security. I'd like to ask you a question between you and me. Did you not say that she has to learn to accept some things? I feel that it is a lot of security to her. I think it is excellent, whether she shows fears or not. I was in a mess that day, but since then I calmed down. After Kathy was in bed, we sort of joked about it. Eventually she'll be the same.

Do you feel, now you know us, do you think that it's both of us? Or do you think that it's just me? That's what's bothering us. We don't know what's behind the fears. We don't know who it is.

I'll tell you what transpired. I was very decisive with her. I just did things. Whether it was right or wrong, I went ahead and told her. I thought she didn't make up her own mind. I felt she's getting away from it to a great degree. She's not a dumb kid. She can use us like mad. Another thing, too. I have told you before when we put the supper on the table she would say, "I don't want it. I don't like it." We say to her, "You sit there until you're ready." She sits for a minute, but then she usually eats it. I think there's a definite improvement. Several things point to it. One thing, she talks about it. She's not indecisive. She doesn't switch. I wish we had ten more like her.

T: You really love her, don't you?

F: Oh, she's a wonderful kid. Basically, she's such a good girl. I've gotten away—my sister has told me I am a perfectionist. I don't know whether that started the fears, but I don't want her perfect. I don't expect her to be perfect. A child can't be perfect. Those things I never realized before. I have never had a child before. Now I know.

I noticed something else I meant to tell you. Sometimes I'm upstairs, and she'll want to come downstairs, and she'll say, "Mommy, I want to take your hand to come downstairs." She'll start to act like she's getting fears. She'll insist in a crying way that it would be her life. She started crying once, and I blew up and slapped her on the rear, and then she went downstairs by herself. I love her. I just love the hell out of her.

T: Your feelings for her are very strong.

F: They couldn't be any stronger. It stems from the fact that I would have such a gorgeous child, such a beautiful kid. To us, she's beautiful. I never thought I would have anything so wonderful. I couldn't find any more happiness with anyone else on this earth.

My wife's love gives me the security I need. It is her undivided, unrestrained relationship with me. She overlooks so many things in me.

T: You really appreciate the way she overlooks your faults.

F: Absolutely.

T: Perhaps you feel you love Kathy too much.

F: No, I don't. I show Kathy all the affection in the world. I pick her up a thousand times, and I play with her. Since the fears, I feel that I have to show Kathy more affection. I've grown into the idea that if I try to show her more love, it will help Kathy do away with her fears. I don't think it would be possible to have too much love. I lacked it myself, the affection part. There couldn't be anything there—not too much of that for a child. I never knew that children could have fears as they do. I'm getting less and less worried about it, and maybe that's helping, too.

January 3. Play Session with Kathy and Mother

C: I can run real, real, real fast.

T: You're a fast runner, hm?

C: See? (*Runs out into hall and then runs back into room.*)

T: Yes.

C: (*Runs in and out of hall again.*)

T: You really like to run.

C: Yes. (*Continues to run back and forth.*) I like to run better than walk. I like to run better.

T: Than walking?

C: Yes. (*Stares at hall.*) A big wolf.

T: Is there a big wolf out there?

C: (*Hands T two puppets.*) You're gonna get these puppets. And Mommy's gonna have these. They aren't the same color. (*Hands two puppets to mother.*) These are so furry. (*Kneels by sandbox. Fills bowl with sand and chops it with a spoon.*) Mommy has a chopping bowl. She uses a big bowl. (*Handles sand.*) You know, when I get undressed for bed, Daddy always brings me surprises.

T: Daddy always brings you surprises when you get undressed for bed?

C: No. He doesn't bring me surprises when I go to sleep at night. He always gives me surprises at dinner. (*Stands up and hands mother a balloon.*) Mommy's gonna get this balloon 'cause she was a good girl, and you're not.

T: I'm bad, hm?

C: Because you were cranky all day.

T: Cranky all day long.

C: (*Spills sand on the floor.*) I gotta find my chopping bowl. All the time I say pooh. Pooh, pooh, pooh.

T: That's just what you feel like saying: pooh.

C: Yeah. (*Runs around the room. Picks up large father doll, then drops it on the floor.*) Throw the little squeaky away. Throwing everything away.

T: You don't like any of them.

C: No. I don't like any of them. (*Tosses a few more toys aside. Picks up shovel and bowl from floor and moves to sandbox. Handles sand.*) Mr. C, you remember I told you when Donna used to throw sand in my eyes.

T: Mm-hm.

C: That made me unhappy. Mommy had to put water in my eyes.

T: That really made you unhappy.

C: Yes. I was unhappy. (*Moves away from sandbox and kicks ball around the room. Pushes comeback. Picks up doll and feeds it with small bottle.*) This has water in it. Drink it. She likes water. She wants it out of the big bottle. (*Picks up large bottle and hands it to T.*) Take the top off. How do you turn it?

T: See?

C: Let me try.

T: It came right off, didn't it?

C: (*Empties small bottle of water into large bottle. Handles the doll.*) It's time for the baby to take her bath. She doesn't like to take her bath.

T: She doesn't like that, does she?

C: No. But she's gonna take one. She doesn't like to stay up by her-self. (*Stuffs doll's diaper into large bottle.*) Baby doesn't like to take her bath.

T: She has to do it anyway.

C: (*Washes the doll with wet diaper.*) I don't care when I take a bath. I like to take a bath.

T: It doesn't bother you at all.

C: No. I don't care if I stay in here all day. I'm a good actor. Aunty Emma's a bad actor. (*Stands up and fills bowl with sand. Chops sand with shovel.*) Mommy's a good actor, and Aunty Emma's a bad girl. She has a big house. Old houses make me sad.

T: Old houses make you sad?

C: Old houses certainly do make me sad.

T: Are you a sad girl?

C: Yes. Because I don't like sad houses. (*Pretends to feed doll some sand.*) Take this, baby. Take it. O.K., take it. See how you like it. Put it back in the bowl. Baby doesn't like chopped liver. I don't want to make no more chopped liver.

T: You don't want to make what baby doesn't eat.

C: Mommy doesn't make the same kind chopped liver. I like chopped liver. Mommy doesn't make this kind.

T: She makes the kind you like.

C: This kind is pooey. Chopped liver is all ready. Put this on the table. (*Empties some water into bowl of sand and rubs sand all over doll's body.*) I never want to play with this again, Mommy.

M: Why not?

C: Because I get myself all dirty. Now baby has to eat. Have to get a towel now. (*Runs to doorway and looks at mother.*) You come with me. (*Mother and C walk out to bathroom.*)

Discussion

Kathy's positive feelings toward her father return. She says, "You know, when I get undressed for bed, Daddy always brings me surprises." At one point, however, Kathy picks up the father-doll figure and throws it hard onto the floor.

Kathy reenacts the feeding situation over and over again, emphasizing that when she does not want to eat certain foods, she will definitely reject them.

January 10. Play Session with Kathy

C: (*Comes into room and pulls chair from around side of workbench. Sits down and pats at clay with stick.*) Get me some water, Mom.

T: You want Mommy to do it for you.

C: Yes. I'll get the other water then. (*Carries clay to pail of water and wets it.*) There. Mommy, get me some water.

M: You can get water yourself, honey.

C: No, I can't!

M: You try.

C: No, you give me some. (*Hands mother the bowl.*)

T: You just want to tell Mommy what to do, hm?

M: Look, I'll show you. (*Mother fills bowl with water from pail. Hands bowl to C, who spills water out of it.*)

C: I want it full. That's not full.

M: You want more water in there? All right. Now you can do it yourself.

C: I want some more.

M: There's this one way you can take it.

C: I want you to get some more out of the sink.

M: No, you get it from here, honey.

C: But there's not enough water. I need some water out of the sink. 'Cause that's not enough!

T: You're pretty mad about it, hm?

C: 'Cause I don't like that kind. (*Fills bowl and slowly carries it to workbench. Sits in chair and pats clay with stick.*) I'm gonna mash it. You just watch what I'm gonna do.

T: O.K.

C: I'm cooking dinner. (*Picks up spoon and jabs at clay with it.*) By the time I get home, my hands will be all dirty. You know, Mr. C?

T: Mm-hm. That's what you're going to do, hm? Get them all dirty.

C: But I won't like that.

T: Don't you like to have your hands dirty?

C: No! It makes me unhappy when I have my hands all dirty. But it doesn't. It doesn't make me unhappy when I get my hands all dirty. I'm gonna make my dolly clean. Where's my cute little dolly? The one with the diaper. Here she is! She wants to take a bath. (*Takes off diaper and lets doll fall on the floor.*) Now the diaper has to get washed. (*Dips diaper into bowl of water and rubs it slowly over the clay.*) I just came here. I don't wanta go home now, 'cause I just came here.

T: You have a lot of things you want to do.

C: (*Picks up doll and handles it with clay-covered hands.*) She has to get real clean, 'cause I told her to. She wants to get clean. I'm gonna wash her. (*Rubs hands with clay and "washes" doll with paper towel.*) I'll get you all cleaned up. All cleaned up. My hands are all full of that stuff. She's gonna get all cleaned up for a birthday party. She's going to a birthday party today. You know? You know, Mommy? My baby's going to a birthday party today.

M: Mm-hm.

C: (*Rubs paper towel over clay and wipes it on doll.*) Her hair is dirty. Her eyes are dirty. And I'm gonna wash her eyes too. You know where Daddy works? Daddy works at ——Company. (*Pause.*) My baby doesn't know how to clean herself. All the time she makes me wash her. She likes me to wash her, 'cause she doesn't know how. All the time she has dirty feet and dirty hands. Now, baby, I'm gonna put you in clean water. In dry water. (*Puts doll into pail of water. Pushes it back and forth in pail.*) Washy-washy, swimmy-swimmy. Swimmy-swimmy, swimmy-swimmy. Get a wash cloth. Clean her off. (*Brings paper towel from workbench and rubs doll vigorously with towel.*) I'll clean her off. Now she's all through taking a bath. I'm gonna dry her. She's soaking wet. (*Marches around the room holding doll. Places doll in sandbox. Steps into box and crouches in sand. Steps out of the sandbox and picks up a hand puppet.*) This bad guy can eat my mommy up.

T: Oh.

C: I don't like that.

T: Don't you like your mommy to be eaten up?

C: No. 'Cause who will take care of him when he goes to work—my daddy?

T: Who would take care of your daddy then, hm?

C: Daddy isn't the girlie. Throw the bad guy away. I'll throw him in the dirt of water. Yeah, I'll throw him in the water. (*Tosses puppet into pail of water.*)

T: That's for the bad guy. Into the water.

C: Yes. Into the water. I don't care if he gets wet. And I'll paintbrush with this. (*Pushes puppet around in pail with a paintbrush.*)

T: That'll take care of him.

C: Yes. (*Continues to push puppet with paintbrush. Picks up another brush and jabs at puppet.*) He's gonna be eaten up. I'll show him. And it's off to bed he goes. And I'm not gonna bring home no surprise for this bad guy. No surprise. Into the water with this bad guy.

T: Nothing for him, hm?

C: Nothing. No supper for him. Into the water with him. (*Lifts puppet out of pail with brush and then lets it drop back into pail. Stirs puppet in the water.*)

T: You're really giving him some pretty bad treatment.

C: Now he's going down the drain and down the drain. You'll see down the drain. 'Cause he's gonna eat me up.

T: He's getting everything he deserves, hm?

C: Yes. But I'm gonna do it to him. I'm gonna drain him down the drain.

T: He'll get just what he gives you, hm?

C: Yes. He's going down and down the drain. (*Throws another puppet into the pail.*) This guy is bad, so I have to drain him down the drain. Most of the guys are mean to me. This guy is mean to me. (*Throws doll from sandbox into pail.*) Every guy is mean to me. Every guy I have to drain down the drain. Every guy is mean to me.

T: Every guy is mean to you.

C: Yes, everyone. Everyone is going down the drain. (*Stirs figures in pail with brush.*)

T: So, you're going to be mean to them.

C: Yes. Everybody drains down the drain. 'Cause everybody drains me down the drain. Everybody doesn't like me.

T: Nobody likes you, hm?

C: All of them are going down the drain. Going down the drain and down the drain. Stick them back down in the water. I'll cut 'em with a knife. With a knife. (*Throws a rubber knife into the pail.*) Stick a knife in the water. That's gonna be very sharp. Here's a gun. This is a ladder. Here's a hammer. And here's a gun! (*Tosses more items into pail. Starts to throw tractor in also but replaces it on table. Stirs items in pail with brush.*) Everybody is mean to me. They don't like me. Everybody doesn't like me. They're all mean to me.

T: Everyone is so mean to you.

C: Yes. The truck is mean to me. Everyone is mean to me. The car is mean to me. Everybody'll drown down the drain.

T: When they're mean to you, that's what you'll do to them.

C: Everyone is so mean to me.

T: Nobody likes you, hm?

C: No! So I'm gonna drain 'em down the drain and drain 'em down the drain. I'll get more water and spill 'em down the drain. (*Empties bowl of water into pail.*) There. Now you're gonna get real sad, and I'll like that.

T: Will you be glad when they're real sad and unhappy?

C: Yes! 'Cause I like 'em to.

T: Mm-hm.

C: Get everything off. This old truck. This gun. (*Throws toys from table on the floor.*)

T: Everything goes, hm?

C: Everything. Everyone is mean to me today. The telephone's ringing. The telephone is dirty. Up and down the numbers. I'm making the numbers wet. (*Dips brush into bottle of water and rubs it over telephone dial.*)

T: Are the numbers naughty, too?

C: They're naughty. The numbers are naughty to me, too. They're naughty to me. That's why I have to make 'em up and down. (*Dips brush into bottle and continues to wet telephone dial.*)

T: This is one time you're going to teach them a lesson.

C: One time I'm gonna teach 'em a lesson. When they get nicer to me, then I'm gonna teach 'em a good lesson. Now how you like that? Now I'm gonna see if I can talk. (*Carries telephone to mother's lap. Holds receiver to ear.*) Hello, Aunty Joan. Hello. Hello. It's my puppet. My dear puppet. It's my dear puppet.

M: Hello, dear puppet.

C: Talk.

M: Oh, I don't know what to say to your puppet. You talk to him.

C: No! I'm not gonna do anything for him. (*Takes telephone from mother and continues to brush it.*) You know what he loves? You know what he told me? He loves me. He loves me. With kisses.

T: He gives you so many kisses because he loves you?

C: Mm-hm. But Aunty Mary is a bad girl.

T: She is?

C: Yes.

T: You don't like her, hm?

C: I'm gonna kick her. And this time I'm gonna kick her.

T: That's what you feel like doing to her, hm?

C: Yes. 'Cause she's a bad girl. I'm gonna hit her over the head. 'Cause I don't like her. Mommy doesn't feel mad at Aunty Mary.

T: She doesn't, but you do.

C: She's going to bed with nothing. I'm gonna throw all of them in the fire. The fire's right out over here. (*Walks to door and throws doll into outer hall.*) There, baby. Now the other kids. (*Throws two puppets into hall.*)

T: You'll throw them all in the fire. Let them burn.

C: This one goes in the fire. The fireman's gonna come and take them away. And throw them away in a fire.

T: They'll be all finished up, won't they?

C: Babies don't like to be burned in the fire.

T: They don't like to be burned, but they are.

C: Yes, but they're burned. I throw mine in the fire. The garbage man's gonna come and put 'em away in a truck. I'm gonna put cuckoo—. I'm gonna make pissy on him. Come on, cuckoo. I'm gonna make pissy on you. (*Goes to doorway and pulls down her pants. Pulls them up again and walks back into room.*) I made pissy on him.

T: You made pissy on him, hm?

C: Yes. Here's another wolf. (*Goes to doorway again and pulls down pants, then pulls them up.*) There.

T: You really are taking care of the wolves today. You pissied right on them.

C: Yes. (*Touches puppets on mother's lap.*) I love these with fur. These are good. They listen to what I say. (*Takes puppets and places them on bench. Lies down on bench, holding puppets.*) They really want to sleep in my bed. They really want to sleep in my bed tonight.

T: They really want to sleep with you.

C: Here comes the flutter. (*Gets up and runs to mother and leans against her. Looks at T.*) Out came the flutter looking for me. My mommy. Then the flutter comes to hit me.

T: Are you afraid of the flutter?

C: Yes.

T: So you run to your mother.

C: Yes. I'm gonna go get my bench. (*Walks to bench and looks at it. Then runs back to mother.*) There's no more flutterbies.

T: No more flutterbies. They're all gone.

C: There's no more. (*Walks to middle of room, then back to mother.*) They weren't all gone.

T: They weren't? There are some there that still bother you, aren't there?

C: There are some nice ones who take care of the bad flutterbies. There's some good flutterbies.

T: There are good flutterbies and bad flutterbies.

C: And the good are—. The king don't like me.

T: Doesn't the king like you?

C: But he always trusts me. I could stay up all night.

T: Is that why you stay up all night?

C: Yes. Oh, splash. (*Throws bottle on the floor and it breaks. Looks startled.*)

T: Well, we'll have to sweep it away so you won't cut yourself, Kathy. I'll just put it out of the way like this now.

C: Now I wanta lay down. (*Stretches out on table, lying on her stomach.*) I really have to lay down. This is my good dress.

T: Mm-hm. Is that the way you like to sleep?

C: Yes. (*Lies on table quietly.*)

T: That's about all the time we have left today, Kathy.

C: I'll be back. Don't forget your coat, Mommy. Good-bye.

T: Good-bye, Kathy.

Discussion

Kathy attempts to get her mother to do things for her, but her mother, unlike previous times, insists that Kathy be responsible for her actions. Kathy's absorption with cleanliness reoccurs.

Kathy throws the "bad guy" into a pail of water and exclaims, "He's gonna be eaten up." She attempts to push the "bad guy" down the drain. Her negative feelings are expanded as she expresses a wish to throw all the human figures down the drain. She exclaims that people are mean to her so she is forced to retaliate. Her feelings increase in intensity as she screams, "I'll cut them all with a knife. With a knife." She shouts, "Everybody is mean to me. They don't like me. Everybody don't like me. They're all mean to me." This is repeated again and again.

Positive perceptions of her father reappear in her comments on the male puppet, "He loves me. He loves me. With kisses." Kathy expresses feelings of resentment toward an aunt, saying, "Aunty Mary is a bad girl . . . I'm gonna kick her . . . I'm gonna hit her over her head."

At the end of the session, Kathy reveals her strength in facing her fears. Directed toward "the cuckoo" and "the wolf," she pulls down her pants and says, "There. I made pissy on them."

January 11. Telephone Conversation with Father

F: My wife wanted me to call you and tell you of an incident that happened in class—the part where she chased a wolf and lowered her pants nicely and sissied on it. She got that from a girl friend. I thought you might want to know that.

   She is going to bed nicely lately. She always wants me to tell her the story of Little Red Riding Hood. She always wants to hear about the wolf chasing Red Riding Hood and the part where the father kills the wolf with an ax.

   She has no fears about the signs any more. I think she's made terrific progress. It makes it much better in our household. She's a cutie. She's got a whole bunch of personality, and she's got brains in her head. We love her so much, and we laugh our heads off with her. In other words, things are going back to a normal shape. Before, we used to be frightened when she talked kind of silly, but now we just laugh with her, and we all have a good time about it. Do you see any point in her continuing to come?

T: Well, I think we should let her make that decision.

F: O.K., then. Whenever she decides that she's had enough, then we'll stop.

January 17. Play Session with Kathy and Mother

C: (*Runs into the room and picks up a balloon.*) You're gonna get the biggest balloon, Mr. C.

T: I'm going to get the biggest one?

C: This is the biggest.

T: O.K.

C: (*Picks up small gun.*) Mommy. (*Walks around the room.*) That bad guy is gonna shoot me. (*Picks up a puppet.*) So you know that's to bed with him. (*Tosses puppet into pail of water.*)

T: Oh, he's going right down into bed.

C: Yes. 'Cause he's so stupid. And so naughty.

T: He's naughty and stupid, hm?

C: And this one is a naughty one. (*Throws another puppet into pail.*) And everyone.

T: Everybody's naughty today, hm?

C: This one, and the horsie is naughty. (*Throws small doll and horse figure into pail.*) Everybody is naughty today. (*Tosses flat figure balloon into pail.*) That stupid old guy! Every time I see him. He's so stupid.

T: He's stupid all the time.

C: Everybody's mean to me. I'm gonna step on him and be an ogre. (*Turns head of Mickey Mouse tractor, then tosses it into pail.*) Put some stuff in his eyes. You hold them, Mommy. (*Picks up a balloon and jumps up and down.*) Jing. I'm gonna sing you a song. First I have to sit down like the girl who is teaching the song. (*Sits down in chair.*)

T: Mm-hm.

C: (*Jumps up from chair and stands near mother.*) You know something? This is gonna be "Jingle Bells."

T: You like that song.

C: Yes. (*Sings "Jingle Bells."*) Always like to dance. (*Sits on chair next to workbench. Dips paintbrush into bottle of water, then smears it on paper.*) I'm pretending I'm painting a house.

T: O.K.

C: You know what house I'm gonna paint? This is gonna be a pink one. It will be a different one.

T: It will be different from any other house, hm?

C: Yes. (*Hums. Rubs brush on clay, then dabs it on paper.*) See what house this is gonna be? See?

T: Mm-hm.

C: (*Hums. Pokes brush into piece of clay.*) I'm pretending that I'm mashing potatoes.

T: Mm-hm.

C: You remember Daddy?

T: I remember him.

C: (*Kneels on chair and looks at T.*) You don't know his last name. His last name is Bernard!

T: Mm-hm.

C: And Mommy's last name is Mrs. Bernard! You know?

T: They both have the same last name, hm?

C: (*Sits in chair again. Dips brush in bottle, then on clay. Brushes some clay on paper.*) I'm making a picture for you. A pretty one. I'm painting a picture for you.

T: Mm-hm.

C: I like you! That's why I'm painting you a picture.

T: Oh, I see.

C: If you were an aunt, then I wouldn't like you. If you were an aunt.

T: You wouldn't like me if I were an aunt?

C: No. (*Handles paper and clay.*) You know what I'm making? A house! That's what I'm making.

T: You seem to like to make houses.

C: I really like to make houses. I feel like it.

T: You feel like making houses?

C: Yes. (*Continues to handle brush and clay. Pokes holes into clay with brush.*) I have to be real quiet, 'cause the cuckoo strikes midnight. Dong! Every time I play with Marcia the cuckoo strikes midnight. Every time I play with Marcia I go to sleep when it's midnight. You know that, Mr. C? And every time the cuckoo strikes midnight when it's morningtime. She's only pretending.

T: Oh, I see. But you go to sleep when she pretends.

C: Yes, when the cuckoo strikes midnight. All the time she says it's morningtime.

T: Mm-hm. She does some pretty funny things, doesn't she?

C: Yes. Every time Marcia says the cockoo strikes midnight, she says, "Go to sleep." 'Cause the cuckoo strikes midnight, and I say "No." And she says, "Do you wanta get hurt?" No.

T: She told you you'd get hurt if you didn't, hm?

C: (*Pauses. Hums.*) Oh, the cuckoo strikes midnight! (*Runs to mother and hugs her.*) Yes, the cuckoo struck. I wanta sit on your lap. (*Sits on mother's lap.*) Oh, lookit my hands.

M: Oh, my goodness.

C: (*Looks at T.*) You know what, Daddy? You know what? Oh! I forgot the wrong name! (*Laughs.*)

T: Mm-hm. You really forgot that time, didn't you?

C: I forgot and said "Daddy." I forgot and said the wrong name.

T: Mm-hm.

C: (*Moves away from mother and picks up jump rope. Twirls it.*) Oh! The cuckoo strikes midnight! (*Runs to mother.*)

T: When the cuckoo strikes midnight, then you run, hm?

C: Yes. (*Sits on mother's lap.*) I don't want Mommy to breathe.

T: Oh, you must want Mommy to stop breathing altogether.

C: Mm-hm. If she doesn't stop, I'll dump her in there in the water and make her sweater get all wet.

T: Is that what you'd like to do?

C: Yes.

T: Dump her right down and get her all wet.

C: (*Picks up jump rope.*) Now, now, I'll just swing it around.

T: You make it go round and round.

C: You know, I won't stop swinging this, 'cause the people go round and round in circles jumping rope.

T: People do funny things sometimes, don't they?

C: Yes. Swingy, swingy. (*Continues to twirl rope while sitting on mother's lap.*) I just love that song. "All I Want for Christmas is My Two Front Teeth"—I like that song. (*Handles jump rope.*) Oh, the cuckoo strikes midnight! Don't want the cuckoo to strike midnight.

T: Are you afraid of the cuckoo striking midnight?

C: Yes. (*Hands jump rope to mother.*) Hold it like this. Like this, Mommy, so the cuckoo won't strike. The cuckoo is falling. (*Takes rope from mother.*) When he hears the cuckoo strike midnight, he runs out of this room.

T: He's afraid of the cuckoo.

C: Yes, he is. I'm stopping the cuckoo. (*Continues to twirl the rope.*)

T: As long as you do that, then the cuckoo stops, hm?

C: Yes. I hear the cuckoo knocking on the window. Knock, knock. I see an ogre gonna eat me up. I'm gonna keep striking this, and the clock is gonna stop. And there's a hoke coming to catch the cuckoo, and he's gonna kill the cuckoo with a stick.

T: And there'll be no more cuckoo, then.

C: Yes. (*Swings jump rope vigorously.*) Cuckoo! Cuckoo, get out of here! I'll make the clock strike, and the cuckoo's gonna eat the ogre up. Dum-dum-dum. Da-da-da-da-da-da. The cuckoo strikes midnight.

T: Mm-hm. You don't like the cuckoo.

C: No. I don't like the ogre, either. I'm gonna get rid of them. (*Swings rope.*) I got rid of the cuckoo and the ogre.

T: You got rid of them both.

C: Let's pretend you're Mom, and you're Daddy, and my other daddy—. I'm gonna pretend I'm Mommy, and you're Daddy, and Daddy's Donna C. (*Looks at T.*)

T: Daddy's Donna C.

C: And do you know Donna C?

T: I only know what you've talked about.

C: Well, I won't talk about her. I'm crumpling the rope up. (*Pulls mother's arm closer around her.*) Do I got a couple more minutes?

T: Oh, yes, you still have a few more minutes.

C: But I don't want to stay here.

T: You don't want to stay?

C: No. I want to go home.

T: You can go home when you want to.

C: I'll stay a few more minutes. (*Pause.*) You know what? Mommy doesn't drive very good.

T: She doesn't?

C: Remember when she smashed the headlights? That's why I have to sit in the back.

T: Mm-hm.

C: (*Hums and handles jump rope.*) I'm gonna gonna show you I can throw you a kiss. (*Sits on mother's lap.*) O.K. (*Points to ball on floor.*) Is this your ball?

T: It belongs in the playroom.

C: I want to take a balloon. Can I take a balloon home?

T: Kathy, all the things have to stay in the room.

C: Why? Why?

T: You wonder why that's necessary.

C: Why, Mr. C?

T: Well, so the other children can play with them. And you can have them to play with next time you come.

C: Next time it'll be here when I come?

T: Mm-hm.

C: When can I go home?

T: You can go home whenever you want to, Kathy. You decide that.

C: Hold me real close.

T: Kathy just wants to be held by Mommy real, real close. Is that it, Kathy?

C: Mm-hm. (*Gets off mother's lap and goes to workbench. Stirs brush in bowl of water.*)

T: Well, I see that your time is up for today, Kathy.

C: O.K. (*Walks out of room with T and mother.*)

Discussion

Kathy mentions the "bad man" in fear, at first, and then with anger. She tosses "him" into a pail of water, calls him stupid and naughty. Her anger spreads as she tosses a number of human and animal figures into the water and shouts, "Everybody's mean to me."

As the session unfolds, Kathy seems happier, not so anxious and tense. She paints freely and enjoys shaping and molding forms with clay. She speaks positively again of her father.

She mentions her night fears and repeats a number of times, "The cuckoo strikes at midnight." This is followed by direct anger expressed against her mother. She yells, "I don't want my mommy to breathe. . . . If she doesn't stop, I'll dump her in there, in the water and make her sweater get all wet." Frequently, Kathy's fears and angry feelings occur simultaneously. Kathy reenacts the night fears over and over again, each time with less intensity.

January 24. Play Session with Kathy and Mother

C: (*Stands in doorway. Walks into room and goes to easel. Pushes brush around in water. Picks up truck and paints it with brush.*) Now I'm gonna paint with a different color. I want it to be black.

T: You want it to be black, hm?

C: Yes, I do. You know what I'm painting, Mommy?

M: What?

C: This color. Color the wheels. (*Puts the truck on floor and picks up a car.*) Those cars. I want to paint something else. I got another truck. I'm gonna paint it another color. Just some of the toys. This is real dirty. (*Paints tractor with brush. Drops tractor and runs back and forth across room.*) The clock struck midnight! The clock struck midnight!

T: The clock struck midnight, hm?

C: Oh, the cuckoo!

T: The cuckoo is coming, so you're running, hm?

C: I don't care. (*Handles nursing bottles. Pours water from small bottle into larger one and carries both to table.*) You gotta be very quiet when the cuckoo strikes midnight. Oh, the cuckoo struck midnight!

T: The cuckoo clock struck midnight again.

C: Mr. Tiptoe is the tiptoe. Oh, look. Little dancing tiptoes! They're chasing me.

T: Do little dancing tiptoes chase you?

C: Yes. And they put me in the fire.

T: Oh, that's what you're afraid of. The fire.

C: (*Paints easel with water. Smiles at T. Puts fingers to mouth.*) Sssh, sssh, sssh.

T: We're going to have to be real quiet, hm?

C: Ssshh. (*Sits on mother's lap and speaks softly to her.*) You know what?

M: What?

C: Be very quiet. 'Cause when the cuckoo strikes midnight, she always plays the game.

M: Hasn't it stopped striking midnight yet?

C: No. When the cuckoo stops striking midnight, I'll fall asleep.

M: You'll fall alseep?

C: On your shoulder.

M: On my shoulder?

C: Yes, on your shoulder. Sssh.

T: You just want everything to be quiet while the cuckoo strikes, hm?

C: I said, "Be quiet." (*Dips paintbrush in water container on easel and paints door with water while sitting on mother's lap.*) I want to sit here.

M: You know, honey, I won't let anything hurt you. You know that, don't you, honey?

C: I said, "Be quiet."

M: Why do we have to be quiet now for?

C: He's gonna hit me.

M: I won't let anything hurt you.

C: I think there's no real cuckoo.

M: You don't think there's a real cuckoo?

C: No. (*Points to male puppets on floor.*) Look at those silly things. Silly men.

T: Silly, silly men. That's what.

C: They wanta bite me.

T: You don't like those men because they'll bite you.

C: Yes. I'm gonna put them in fire. They'll be sorry, and they'll never come back again.

T: Mm-hm. Burn them right up.

C: Yes. And they can never come back again. (*Stands up and gets animal puppets.*) Not these puppets. These puppets are good to me.

T: They're the only good ones, hm?

C: Yes. 'Cause they have fur.

T: You like the fur ones.

C: Yes, I do. (*Again sits on mother's lap. Hums.*) Tickle me. Tickle me! (*Laughs.*) Tickle my hair.

M: Not now, honey.

C: Tickle my hair! Tickle my hair! I'm gonna stamp on you, Mom. (*Gets down from mother's lap and stamps her feet.*) I don't want to yell at Mommy. Mommy doesn't yell.

T: Doesn't your mommy yell at you?

C: No. Sometimes she does when I'm mean, and sometimes she doesn't.

T: Mm-hm. When you're mean, then Mommy yells at you.

C: Yes. She yells real loud. (*Handles puppet.*) Let's see inside the puppet. Inside the puppet. (*Peers inside the puppet.*) See in the puppet. This puppet. The cuckoo strikes midnight. I don't want to stay here now.

T: You don't have to stay, Kathy. You're the one who decides that. It's up to you. You can go whenever you want to go.

C: I want to go upstairs, Mommy.

M: You don't want to stay here anymore?

C: No.

T: O.K., Kathy.

C: Leave these here. (*Puts puppets on the floor.*) What's in there? (*Points to mother's purse.*)

M: You know what's in there, honey.

C: What?

M: All my things.

C: Gum?

M: You're not getting any more gum today.

C: Is there gum in there?

M: No.

C: Let me smell.

M: No, I said, honey.

C: Let me smell something. I want to smell something.

M: No, honey.

C: I want to smell something. (*Hits mother and pulls at her skirt.*)

T: Mommy just won't let you do it.

M: Kathy. Are you having fun hitting me?

C: I'm gonna pull her skirt.

T: You're really mad at Mommy.

C: I'm gonna tear her skirt.

M: Is that what you want to do?

C: Yes.

M: Kathy. Would you like me to pull you like that?

C: No.

M: Well, all right.

C: If you pull my socks down, if you hit me and kick me and kick me, then I'll hit you. I wanta look in your purse.

M: I'll let you look in my purse when we get in the car. I don't want you to take it apart now.

C: Smell it.

M: You can smell it and everything else later.

T: If Mommy doesn't let you do what you want to do, then you get angry.

C: Those silly guys. I'm gonna throw them in the fire, where they belong. (*Throws male puppets into pail of water.*) Going down the water drain. These silly things are going in.

T: All of them are going in. Just what they deserve.

C: I don't want to put them in, but they got dirt. (*Places puppets to one side. Throws a small car into the pail.*) He's mean. And this little dolly's mean. Put them in the water.

T: So many mean ones.

C: Yes. So many, so many. The water's mean. (*Empties nursing bottles into pail.*)

T: Even the water is mean to you.

C: And the bottles are mean to me. (*Drops bottles into pail.*) And this water is mean to me. This is mean to me. (*Continues to throw toys into pail.*) Everything is mean to me. Everything is mean to me today.

T: Everything is mean to you.

C: Yes. This, and this. They're all mean. This airplane's mean. Nothing is nice to me.

T: They're all mean to you.

C: Yes. Together with the bad wolf.

T: Together with the bad wolf, hm?

C: That bad wolf. (*Takes the paddle out of the canoe.*) I want to scoop with this for a delicious dinner. And scoop a delicious dinner. This isn't mean to me. This is a scoop for a delicious dinner.

T: Kathy, you just have a few more minutes left to play today.

C: But I want to stay here. (*Eats more sand and spits on floor.*) I'm gonna stay here, and then I'll make bread and butter.

T: Then you'll make bread and butter?

C: Mm-hm. I just love bread and butter. I'm gonna spit down the water drain. (*Walks to drain and spits on floor. Peers down drain. Eats sand and handles paddle.*) I just got here, Mr. C. I just came here.

T: You just arrived right now.

C: I don't want to go home now.

T: You'd like to stay, hm? Well, there are just a couple minutes left.

C: But I don't feel like going home.

T: You feel like staying here?

C: Mm-hm. You know when I'm going to leave? Tomorrow.

T: You want to stay until tomorrow.

C: Yes. You know what doesn't bother me?

T: What doesn't bother you?

C: The chewing-gum sign. The one with the man. I'll empty my food all out. (*Throws bowl into pail after emptying sand into sandbox.*) There. Now. Good-bye, Mr. C.

T: Good-bye, Kathy.

Discussion

Kathy begins the session by painting. Her attention span in the playroom is longer, and she is more persistent in achieving her goals. Her repetitive questions have disappeared, and she is more independent of her mother.

Her fears appear again, but the feelings are much less intense. Kathy's behavior is more like a game than an expression of real fear. She says, "I don't care" (about the cuckoo), and later, "When the cuckoo strikes midnight, she always plays the game." Kathy's mother accepts Kathy's strange actions, reassures her, "You know, honey, I won't let anything hurt you."

Kathy becomes hostile again, attacking the male puppets and throwing them into the "fire." She shouts, "I'm gonna stamp at you, Mom." Then, more sensitively, "I don't want to yell at Mommy. Mommy doesn't yell."

Kathy attacks "the silly guys" again and throws them into a pail of water. She throws the doll figures and some of the toys in the water, exclaiming, "Everything is mean to me today." Kathy also throws the "bad wolf" into the water too. Her fears are diminishing, both in nature and in intensity, in the playroom.

January 31. Play Session with Kathy and Mother

C: (*Runs to chair and pulls it in front of workbench. Puts clay on sheet of paper. Picks up male puppets.*) They're stupid.

T: Those are the stupid ones, hm?

C: Yes. And this is stupid. And this is stupid. (*Drops puppets into pail of water. Also throws a tractor and a diver figure into pail.*) They're all stupid today. They're going down the water drain.

T: They're going right down.

C: (*Picks up animal puppet and then drops it on the floor.*) I'm not even gonna talk to him. 'Cause he's not nice to me.

T: He isn't?

C: He didn't be nice to me today. He's the bad man.

T: And are you afraid of the bad man?

C: No. (*Throws toys from table on to floor.*) This is a stupid old car. This is a stupid old boat.

T: They're all stupid, hm?

C: Stupid old automobile. It's stupid. Do you know they're stupid?

T: Mm-hm. Every one of them just plain stupid.

C: That stupid shovel. (*Continues to throw toys on the floor.*) That's a stupid airplane, too.

T: You don't like stupid things.

C: N-O! (*Hits her mother.*)

T: You feel like hitting Mommy, hm?

C: I don't like you.

M: Why?

C: N-O!

M: Do you want to tell Mommy why you're hitting her?

C: You know why?

M: Why?

C: I'm gonna get some paint on you. (*Rubs paintbrush on mother's skirt.*)

M: Did you get mad at me for something, honey?

C: I'm hungry. That's why I'm hitting you.

M: You're hungry? You just had a sandwich and five cookies.

C: (*Continues to hit at mother's skirt with brush.*) You bad boy. You bad girl. I don't like you.

M: But I like you. You like to hit Mommy?

C: Where's that little tea? That little cup? That cup. Here it is. You know why I need it? I need it for something.

T: Mm-hm.

C: I'm gonna put it in this water. (*Drops cup into water container on easel. Dips brush into water and paints on paper and easel.*) I'm painting something. (*Sighs. Continues to paint easel with water. One brush falls to the floor a few times.*) That stupid old paintbrush. That I don't like.

T: You don't like stupid things.

C: That stupid old paintbrush is always falling. I'll leave it there. (*Goes to workbench and pours water from nursing bottle over clay. Pours more water on clay and watches it trickle down bench to floor.*) For God's sakes!

T: It really splattered all over, hm?

C: God O mighty! Did you ever hear anything like that?

T: God all mighty?

C: Keep quiet! N-O, Mr. C.

T: O.K. That's the way you want it.

C: (*Throws animal puppet into pail of water*.) This one's been naughty, so I'll put him in a bath. Everybody is naughty today. (*Pokes in clay with paintbrush*.) Is that all today? Do I go home pretty soon?

T: Well, you still have about eight more minutes, Kathy.

C: O.K. But I just came here.

T: It seems as though you just came, hm?

C: Now I'm gonna make something else. (*Sighs*.) What I make now? (*Handles doll figures*.) What's in that big bag? Stuff, I guess. Gonna stand him up. (*Stands male doll upright*.) They're all stupid today.

T: Everybody is stupid.

C: N-O. Don't talk about it. (*Walks back to workbench. Pokes brush into clay*.) I'm gonna make something else now. I changed my mind. I wanted to make a blueberry pie.

T: Mm-hm.

C: (*Turns handle of vise with clay-covered hands*.) I'm getting this so dirty that you could hardly paint no more.

T: Just one more minute left, Kathy, and then you have to stop for today.

C: O.K. But first I gotta go wash my hands. I'm all through. Now I want to leave right now.

T: O.K. You want to leave now.

C: (*Walks out of the room with mother*.)

Discussion

Kathy continues to express angry feelings toward the male puppets and "the bad man" and indicates that she is no longer afraid of "him." She hits her mother and says, "I don't like you," then tries to paint her.

The angry feelings that Kathy shows toward her parents in the play situation are more direct, but milder. She expresses a great deal of positive feeling toward them and shares numerous positive identifications.

Kathy exhibits no fear in this play session. She moves freely, is unconcerned about cleanliness, and paints spontaneously. She indicates, in her frequent questions about remaining time, that the play therapy experience does not continue to have the same value for her.

February 6. Telephone Conversation with Father

F: I called you to see if there was anything you wanted to know.

T: Was there something particular you had in mind?

F: Everything is pretty doggone good. Of course, the fears don't all leave right away. They're diminishing, though. Her progress is really noticeable.

   By the way, I wanted to tell you one thing. One night on a television program a Mr. C was on, and someone said, "How do you do, Mr. C?" She turned to me and said "I know Mr. C."

February 14. Play Session with Kathy and Mother

C: (*Runs into room and picks up balloons.*) These are my favorite balloons.

T: You really like those, hm?

C: Yes. And this yellow one for you.

T: It's for me, hm?

C: No. The yellow one's for Mommy. This is her favorite balloon. There. Here, Mommy. (*Also hands T a balloon.*) Here for you. If I don't eat my supper, Daddy doesn't bring me any surprises. I just have to eat my supper. (*Looks at mother.*) Tell him about I don't eat my supper. O.K.? Tell him that.

M: You mean when Daddy says he's got a surprise, and you find out, and you don't want to eat, and you say you want your surprise right then? Daddy says you should eat your supper first, doesn't he?

C: Yeah. You tell him.

M: I did tell him.

C: Well, tell him now!

M: Again?

C: Yes.

M: Well, Kathy doesn't eat her supper, and Daddy comes home and has a surprise for her. And Daddy says, "Well, you can't have your surprise then, if you don't eat your supper."

C: (*Starts to turn a somersault, then stops.*) I don't want to do one. Is my daddy new?

M: He's the only daddy you have.

C: He *is* new. (*Picks up a car and covers it with sand.*)

T: Kathy, you just have a short while longer left for today.

C: I still want to play some more. O.K.?

T: You still want to play some more, hm?

C: Yes.

T: Well, you still have a little more time.

C: O.K., Mr. Clocky-pocky. (*Walks to dollhouse and handles some doll furniture. Also plays with small doll figure.*) The little baby sits down at her table. And here's her breakfast.

T: We'll have to stop for today, Kathy.

C: O.K. (*Feeds each doll a little more sand. Gets up and walks out of the room, followed by mother and T.*)

Discussion

Kathy expresses positive feelings toward her mother, giving her the favorite balloon. She plays through the mealtime situation again, but with less intense feelings and reactions. She accepts the fact that unless she eats her dinner, there will be no surprises and does not confuse this rule with loss of love and status. She asks her mother to state her father's rule. Kathy asks, "Is my daddy new?" and then, "He *is* new." Here Kathy is referring to her father's new, patient approach and consistency in setting limits.

February 21. Kathy Terminates her Therapy

On this day Kathy started to walk down to the playroom and suddenly stopped. She looked at the therapist and said, "I don't want to come here and play any more." "All right, Kathy," the therapist responded, "that's up to you." Kathy said, "N-O, N-O, N-O." She went up the steps, smiled, waved good-bye to the therapist, and walked away with her mother.

May 15. Interview with Mother and Father

About three months later, Mr. and Mrs. Bernard arranged for a brief talk with the therapist and reported the following:

F: We just came in to tell you that Kathy has just had her adenoids taken out.

M: Yes, and she was really wonderful. Some of the other children yelled and screamed and cried, but Kathy just went in quietly and went through the operation without a whimper.

F: When we told her we wouldn't be able to stay in the hospital with her, she just accepted it. She's a wonderful kid. We're very proud of her.

M: We told her we would be in to see her early in the morning, and then she could go home. When we took her to the hospital we sort of made a game out of it, and she joined right in.

F: We explained very simply what would happen while she was in the hospital, and she thought that would be fun.

Well, we don't want to take any more of your time. Kathy has been fine at home, just fine. She's been going to sleep without trouble and doesn't wake up at night, and there hasn't been any sign of her fears.

M: And she's doing everything she used to do, and she's so much happier. We're really grateful that she had the opportunity to come for play therapy and that we brought her here right at the beginning when the fears first started.

F: Well, we'd better go. Thanks again.

T: I've enjoyed working with you and Kathy very much. It's been a pleasure knowing you. So long.

M: Good-bye and thank you, Mr. C.

Concluding Comments on Kathy's Play Therapy Experiences

Kathy's experiences in relationship play therapy helped her to achieve more realistic and acceptable interactions with her parents. She realized that they loved her.

She expressed her anxieties and inner conflicts over and over again. Her struggles to suppress her anger toward her parents aroused frustration and tension and contributed to her bizarre and marked fear reactions. The anger itself was the outcome of numerous family pressures on her—cleanliness, food, toilet training. Kathy perceived these pressures to mean that her parents' love was conditional.

As Kathy began to feel secure in the therapeutic relationship, and accepted and respected by the therapist, she became able to project her angry feelings in various play fantasies and creations. At first, the angry feelings were indirect and subtle. In time, however, she focused them directly toward her parents and expressed them repeatedly in a number of different ways.

Kathy's strange fears disappeared and her anger became milder in intensity. She relaxed in the playroom, played in a more focused way, and was no longer obsessed by a need for perfect cleanliness. She played freely and spontaneously with sand, water, and paints.

At the same time, her parents eased their pressures on Kathy. They accepted her perceptions of people and things. They attempted to understand her feelings, and responded to her more compassionately.

The play therapy experience and the contributions of her parents in bringing about new family relationships helped Kathy to achieve positive attitudes toward herself and her parents and to value more highly her own way of being.

8

Implications of Therapy Outside the Playroom

*C*hildren grow as persons in and through their relationships with significant others in their lives. Observations and transcriptions of tape-recorded child–therapist interactions in play therapy consistently have pointed to the importance of trust, acceptance, and respect. Relationship play therapy offers methods of communication and therapist responsiveness that can be learned and applied by parents and teachers in facilitating creative learning and problem resolution.

Attending to children's verbal expressions and body language, conveying understanding, and providing opportunities for emotional expression have stood out in my experience as effective ways of facilitating child self-disclosure, growth, and development. Qualitative listening includes interest in, attention to, and concern for the individual child. It means being sensitive to nuances in children's feelings, catching the essence of definiteness, clarity, confusion, inconsistency, subtlety, and ambivalence. The challenge for the listener is to come into touch with the core or essence of the child's attitudes. As parents and teachers develop an empathic, listening attitude, they are guided by questions such as: "What feelings is this child expressing now?" "What, essentially, is this child conveying?" Sensitivity and responsiveness to children's interests and feelings can become a natural part of adult–child relationships.

Feeling understood, accepted, and respected, children reveal more of their inner feelings. As they do, they develop a sense of security with adults and become motivated to talk more about their real selves. They gain clearer, more realistic self-perceptions. In the process, they share what dominates their inner life. When listened to, children become freer and more expressive, more truly themselves. They disclose the qualities of their being.

Any interested person may become an empathic listener and a valid communicator of emotional understanding. In assisting children to grow emotionally, listening, empathizing, and conveying understanding of feelings occur in ongoing communications between adult and child.

Unstructured Media: Adult Applications

Unstructured play materials are an important resource in helping children express their interests and feelings. Media such as clay, finger paints, sand, and water facilitate dramatic creations. Other valuable play materials include dolls and doll furniture, puppets, rubber knives and guns, scissors and paper, crayons, balloons, large comeback toys, and nursing bottles. These may be used by children in spontaneous dramatic play, free associations, and role playing.

Some children use these media to express joy, happiness, and good will; others use them to work out hostilities and resentments. Jealously, anxiety, and hatred may be projected onto inanimate objects in an effort to come to terms with difficult relationships and move toward creative paths.

Through play, children may act out perceptions of self, family, and others in ways that would not be revealed in the everyday world. Imaginary expressions enable children to cope with insecurities that arise in the world of reality. Children should be given time and a place with play materials, opportunities to smear and mess, to draw and paint, to create and destroy, to engage in dramas involving their families and others in society.

While play itself frequently offers emotional release to children, it is not automatically accompanied by insight. The presence of an adult whose aim is to help children clarify their feelings and be themselves is an important requisite and hastens the process of resolving emotional tensions and conflicts. Children should not be forced to play. The decision should be left to the child. Further, children should not be pressured into using materials as defined by others. The play materials have different meanings to different children and their use should not be directed by social definitions. Children should be free to explore their own symbolic interpretations and meanings. The inner process that a child experiences in making decisions and in personalizing play materials is in itself a growth process contributing self-knowledge and affirmation.

From the above principles, a number of guides can be derived, which adults may find useful in their contacts with children:

1. Some provision should be made for a selected quantity and variety of play materials, both structured and unstructured, so that the child is free to select the type or quantity of material needed or wanted.
2. Children should be encouraged to verbalize their feelings.
3. Children should decide for themselves how they want to use the materials.
4. Children should be permitted to express what they wish directly and in play and not be obliged to follow a social standard.
5. Adults should respond to children's silent and verbal expressions of feelings, and in some way indicate understanding and acceptance of them.
6. Adults should not interpret to the child the symbolism involved in play. Unless the adult makes the correct interpretation (an interpretation which coincides with the child's meaning at that moment), the adult may generate untimely and unconnected feelings rather than aid the child in expressing what is immediately alive. The child's own perceptions and statements provide the best clues to meaning and these should be accepted as expressed.

The Experiences of Mrs. A

Some time ago I gave a talk to a small group of mothers, during which I presented ways to understand children's feelings and support their self-actualizing tendencies. Mrs. A, one of the mothers present in the group, later made an appointment with me. During our interview, Mrs. A stated that she had never clearly understood Betty, her 8-year-old daughter. In her words, "I have never really tried to understand her feelings, I guess. Maybe it was because I was afraid of them. But now I want to try and help her express her feelings more easily. I know she keeps so much to herself." Approximately four months later, Mrs. A reported the following:

"You won't believe it, but quite a bit has happened to me. When I left your office, I was a very determined person, but I ran into all kinds of stumbling blocks. First of all, Betty wouldn't talk about her feelings. At least I could not detect them or clearly follow her. Then one day I made a decision. I had been on the verge of carrying it out before and had thought about it a hundred times. I went to my parents' house. I told them I had something to say to them and I wanted to say it privately. I took them into the kitchen and closed the doors and told them to sit down. I think it was the hardest thing I ever did. They looked at me in a puzzled way and wondered what in the world I wanted. After about two minutes' silence, while I was struggling to hold onto myself, I finally said the words: 'I want you to know that there were many times in my life when I hated you both. I couldn't say it then, but you said many things to me and did many things to me which really hurt me, and I hated you for them.'

"Then I poured it all out to them, relating some of the incidents which had particularly affected me. To my amazement, they listened, and they listened with understanding. They let me talk it out. You don't know how wonderful that made me feel. They told me that there were times when they hated me, too, and for the first time I was aware that I was listening to their feelings. When they were through talking, we all cried, and we knew that we really loved each other. For the first time, I believe, we could be thoroughly honest in expressing our feelings toward each other, and since then we have been much happier people.

"After this incident, I seemed to be a different person. I began to see many feelings in Betty that I never knew existed before. I had not seen how compulsive she had been about cleanliness, yet she had been telling me in so many ways for such a long time that she was afraid to get dirty. I wrote down some things that she had said to me each day for a few weeks, and there in my notes were her fears, holding her in, preventing her from being free and warm and friendly with other children. . . .

"So I bought some finger paints and plenty of paper, and I put a large table in the backyard. We sat down together, and I said to Betty, 'Now let's make the messiest picture we possibly can.' At first, it was very difficult for her. She was reluctant. She was afraid to even touch the paints, and I didn't force her. It was difficult for me, too. I never imagined it would be so hard to smear paints. In a sense, we learned to do it together, and it released a lot of the feeling inside. . . .

"As time went on, Betty began to express some of her feelings more clearly. I encouraged her to go ahead and talk about them, even though sometimes what she said was somewhat critical of me and her father. It was hard to take, but I continued to accept her feelings nonetheless, and little by little I felt her feelings change. I felt my own feelings change, too.

"It was exciting to watch Betty become freer not only at home but also in the neighborhood. She became friends with some of the children on the block and invited them to the house. She played with her baby brother more and kissed him and showed him more affection. One day, she set up a table in the yard, and they finger painted together. This was the first time she has ever shown him much attention. . . .

"Her paintings changed, too. When the messy painting first started, I thought it would last just a short time, and then for a while I wondered if it wouldn't continue forever. But it changed, and she began to make very beautiful designs and wonderful arrangements of form and color.

"Betty has shown improvement in many ways. She is much warmer and affectionate toward me. It's like having a new relationship with someone you've known a long time. We're more secure with each other. I'm not so critical of her anymore. I just let her be herself. It's been a wonderful experience for me. We've grown together, and I know we'll continue to grow in this way. . . ."

Mrs. A was able to utilize in her family the philosophy, concepts, and guides of relationship play therapy. She was able, in her own way, to work out difficult emotional patterns with her parents and with her daughter. The process was not an easy one. It involved a strong emotional struggle and inner motivations, which were maintained and strengthened in spite of many threatening setbacks.

What happened to Mrs. A and Betty may be considered a normal growth experience which had been temporarily shut off by harbored fears and insecurities. As Mrs. A renewed her faith in herself as a competent mother, and as she accepted her attitudes toward her parents and respected her own judgments and values, she became free of inhibiting emotions. She was able to create a different kind of relationship with Betty. And in this warmth and inner peace, mother and daughter finally understood and accepted each other, becoming happier and more creative in their interpersonal relations in the family and in an expanded social world.

References

Axline, V. (1950). Play therapy experiences as described by child partici-
pants. *Journal of Consulting Psychology* 14(1):53–63.

Mott Foundation (1996). *A Fine Line: Losing American Youth to Violence.*
Flint, MI.

Moustakas, C. (1953). *Children in Play Therapy.* New York: McGraw-
Hill.

——(1959). *Psychotherapy with Children: The Living Relationship.* New
York: Harper & Bros.

——(1975). *Who Will Listen?* New York: Ballantine.

——(1981). *Rhythms, Rituals and Relationships.* Detroit, MI: Center for
Humanistic Studies.

Rank, O. (1936). *Will Therapy and Truth and Reality.* New York: Knopf.

Taft, J. (1933). *The Dynamics of Therapy in a Controlled Relationship.*
New York: Macmillan.

Index